CONNE**CT**ECHNIQUE

The first creativity technique for screenwriters

Lajos Tribl

Translated by Edwin Miles

Frankfurt 2023

DEAR READER,

as writers, you probably know the problem: you are working on a story but have run out of ideas for how to move it forward, which can naturally be extremely frustrating. Some people call it writer's block, others perhaps a lack of talent. Lajos Tribl calls it a lack of a system. But whichever way you turn it, at the end of the day the sufferer is left with no ideas to work with.

To overcome this problem, Lajos has developed the story element system (category system) and the connect technique (creativity technique). Despite the fact that the system is simple, it is very effective for creating stories. You'll be amazed at what you can do with this new tool — the Swiss Army knife for storytelling.

I hope you enjoy reading *Connect Technique* and wish you every success with your projects.

Rafael Jovanovic
Film composer

AT A GLANCE

Illustrations: Lajos Tribl. Translated from German by Edwin Miles. This book was typeset using Adobe InDesign CS6.

Bibliographic information of the German National Library: The German National Library lists this publication in the German National Bibliography; detailed bibliographic data are available on the Internet at dnb.dnb.de.
Copyright © 2023 by Lajos Tribl.
Production and publisher: BoD – Books on Demand, Norderstedt
ISBN: 9783757819927

NOTE

Who this book is for

This book is intended for storytellers. A comprehensive analysis of *Jaws* (one of the best-structured films ever made) and other films forms the basis of the material presented here. The book is suitable:
— as a textbook for film schools and seminars;
— for self-study.

What this book does

The first chapter introduces the eleven different elements of the story element system (SES). Chapter 2 shows how I use the story element system as a basis for a creativity technique – with the connect technique you can create countless scenes for a story. In chapters 3 and 4, I will demonstrate how authors can utilize the story element system to structure and analyze stories, with several different examples. You will find tips and tricks for working with the SES in chapter 5.

Note

The book is designed to be easily readable throughout. However, there are a few pages that require a higher level of concentration and attention to detail. The example stories I've created have been kept simple and are intended only to show the techniques presented here as clearly as possible. You won't find a Shakespeare here, I'm afraid, but you will encounter an offbeat sense of humor.

Introduction

Every film consists of single actions. Each of these actions fulfills a particular purpose in the story. You can compare a single action with a jigsaw puzzle piece. The single puzzle pieces join to form the finished story. An example of a single action can be found in *Jaws*: Mrs. Kintner wants someone to kill the shark. *Enemy of the State* also contains the single action *a character wants something*: Reynolds wants the video of the murder. The single action *a character wants something* represents an important puzzle piece in many films and is one of eleven categories I have encountered in my in-depth film analyses — every film contains at least several of the different categories, while some contain all of them. You know each of these categories, but so far no one has come up with the idea of developing a category system from them. I call this category system the *story element system*. This system forms the foundation for the first creativity technique developed for the film industry. With this system, writers are able not only to create stories, but also to analyze them. To analyze a story, a writer categorizes every single action as one of these eleven elements. The aim is to detect flaws in the story development, flaws that exist because elements have either not been used or have been used in the wrong way.

Let's take a look at an example
We take a walk through the city and observe our fellow human beings' behavior. We might see the following:
— Nico, cursing, exits an office building.
— Franca consoles her crying son, Renzo.
For the purposes of analysis, we categorize these two actions as elements:

— we categorize Nico's behavior as the element *emotional re-action* (ER). What is an ER? An emotional reaction to an event, for example a catastrophe.
— we categorize Franca's action as the element CPAC.

What is a CPAC? CPAC is short for *carrying out the plan against a catastrophe*. We use a CPAC to counteract a catastrophe. Example: catastrophe: Adriano drops a glass on the floor and it breaks. PAC (*plan against a catastrophe*): Adriano *wants* to sweep up the shards of glass. A PAC is a plan/idea that refers to wanting to do something to counteract the catastrophe. Often, a PAC contains the expression *wants*. CPAC (Adriano carries out his plan): he sweeps up the glass. If Adriano is wealthy, his PAC might look like this: Adriano *wants* his butler to sweep up the broken glass. CPAC: cursing softly to himself (ER) because he just had to wash Adriano's socks, the butler sweeps up the glass.

The scene *the nice Franca consoles a crying Renzo* consists of two elements:
Element #1 (ER): Renzo cries.
Element #2 (CPAC): Franca consoles Renzo.
We can also subdivide Renzo's sadness into two elements:
Element #1: for Renzo, his sadness is an *emotional reaction*.
Element #2: for Franca, Renzo's sadness is a *catastrophe*.

Logically, what does a loving mother do when faced by such a *catastrophe*? She reacts with a PAC: she wants to console her son. CPAC: she consoles Renzo. But what was the *catastrophe* that triggered Renzo's sadness? He accidentally dropped his ice cream on the ground. A caring mother naturally thinks of an additional PAC after she has consoled her son: Franca wants to buy

Renzo a fresh ice cream. CPAC: Franca goes to the ice cream van with her son to ask for a new one. *Catastrophe*: Renzo's favorite ice cream is sold out. How does Renzo react to this *catastrophe*? His ER might look like this: in his anger, Renzo kicks the ice cream van, leaving a dent. Renzo is actually 40 years old and not in control of his emotions. Practice makes perfect: sketch out several possible ER scenes for Renzo. Each ER should reflect a different underlying mentality.

In a properly structured story, each individual element plays an important role as a segment within the overall plot. The acid test is whether, by removing the segment in question, we damage the overall sense of the story. By categorizing a single action, we become more aware of the role the single action plays in the story. A single action that has been categorized can also be tackled more directly in further story development. This strategy represents a new approach to storytelling:

— Single action: Nico loses his well-paid job. By categorizing this action as the element *catastrophe*, we can develop the scene more specifically by asking questions: what element could follow a *catastrophe*?
— Perhaps an *emotional reaction*: Nico hurls his briefcase angrily onto the sidewalk outside the office building. An ER like this, however, would only make sense for office workers who are not in control of their emotions.
— We can try an ER that is more appropriate for an emotionally mature person: cursing quietly to himself, Nico leaves the company headquarters behind, swearing revenge. This scene contains two elements: Nico curses quietly to himself = ER. Nico wants revenge = PAC.

— Which *plan against a catastrophe* (PAC) could advance the story? Nico wants to look for a new job? No, he doesn't want that. It's not dramatic enough. The audience demands a stronger, more dramatically effective element:

— PAC: Nico wants to rob a bank. The robbery calls for the element *preparation*.

— PR (*preparation* — Nico prepares the CPAC [the robbery]): at the central train station, he buys a pistol illegally (1) and practices firing it in the woods (2). We tie an additional *catastrophe* for Nico to the first part of the *preparation*:

— Catastrophe: police officers spot him buying the pistol illegally. For the cops, however, the previous observation of Nico is not a *catastrophe*, but rather a CPAC in response to their own *catastrophe*: They see Nico talking to several shady-looking men at the train station, an interaction the cops judge to be suspicious. Nico manages to escape the cops.

With the help of the various elements, writers are unerringly able to build their story by starting with a single action and developing additional ones. Chess players visualize the game ahead and mentally try out every possible move until they find one that works. Writers, similarly, will try out various elements on a single action until they find a suitable one — see Chapter 2. In this book, I introduce the eleven different elements. With this category system, screenwriters think through a scene down to the finest detail and develop it further. The system is essentially invisible to viewers because they live in one themselves:

— PAC: Jim wants to drive to work.
— Preparation: shower. Brush teeth. Eat breakfast.
— Catastrophe: no milk in the refrigerator.

— ER: Susan is annoyed at Jim, her husband, because he hasn't bought any milk.
— CPAC: Jim drives to work.
— Catastrophe: traffic jam.
— ER: now it's your turn: come up with three ER scenes, preferably three unconventional ones.

Our lives, newspaper reports, novels, films including *Jaws* consist of elements. Let's take a closer look at *Jaws*:

Jaws

is a masterpiece of film structure and is consistently told. What does *consistently told* mean? The film contains no unnecessary actions (elements) that drag it out — see page 95—96: *Detecting development faults* and *Find the mistake.*

The plot of Jaws

A seven-meter great white shark kills Chrissie Watkins close to the beach town of Amity. Because the mayor refuses to close the beach, the shark kills three more people. Brody, Hooper and Quint, a local shark hunter, head out to sea on a decrepit old boat in an attempt to kill the shark, but the shark turns the tables and hunts their boat, attacking it until it falls apart and sinks.

Note

BB is an abbreviation for *building block*, a time interval in the film. BB 09:14—11:05 is the interval 09:14—11:05 in the film. Building blocks are also used in this book without seconds. Example: BB 9—11 — see pages 16—19.

Act 1: start—21:39
BB 01:11—02:22: Chrissie and other students are having fun at
a beach party (ER).
BB 02:22—03:27: Chrissie goes swimming in the sea (CPAC) —
see page 84 4.3.
BB 03:27—04:55: A great white shark kills Chrissie (*catastrophe*).
BB 04:55—06:49: Brody wants to check Chrissie's remains (PAC)
that have been discovered (*catastrophe*).
BB 06:49—08:33: Brody drives to the beach and checks the remains (CPAC).
BB 08:33—09:14: On the phone, Brody learns that a shark
killed Chrissie (*catastrophe*). Brody wants to
close the beach (PAC).
BB 09:14—11:05: Brody purchases the items and equipment he
needs to close the beach (*preparation*).
BB 11:05—13:03: Brody doesn't achieve his goal of closing the
beach.
BB 13:03—15:55: People are lying on the beach, and several
are swimming in the sea.
BB 15:55—17:28: The shark kills Alex Kintner — act climax.
BB 17:28—19:45: Town hall meeting. Mrs. Kintner wants someone to kill the shark. Brody wants to close the
beach.
BB 19:45—21:39: We meet Quint. Locals close the beach.

Act 2: 21:39—69:40
BB 21:39—23:31: The hunt begins: Brody reads books about
sharks.
BB 23:31—26:34: Two men set baits for the shark.
BB 26:34—29:45: People from both Amity and from outside set

out to hunt down the shark. We get to know
Hooper.

BB 29:45—31:27: Hooper examines Chrissie's remains. At the
same time, some men catch a tiger shark,
which we don't see because we are with
Hooper, who announces that a shark killed
Chrissie.

BB 31:27—33:31: People celebrate the dead tiger shark.

BB 33:31—34:39: Hooper believes they've got the wrong shark
— he wants to cut it open.

BB 34:39—36:25: Mrs. Kintner blames Brody for Alex's death.
Brody feels guilty for his role in Alex's death.

BB 36:25—37:51: Brody is depressed because he feels responsible for Alex's death.

BB 37:51—39:35: Hooper visits Brody. We get to know Hooper
better.

BB 39:35—41:43: Hooper tells Brody that the killer shark is still
alive. Hooper and Brody want to cut the tiger-
shark open.

BB 41:43—43:28: Hooper cuts the tiger shark open and proves
that the killer shark is still alive. As a result,
Hooper wants to go after the killer shark.
Brody wants to close the beach.

BB 43:28—45:16: Brody and Hooper go out to sea on a boat.

BB 45:16—48:19: Hooper finds Ben Gardner's body in the sea.

BB 48:19—51:20: The mayor wants to reopen the beach even
though the killer shark is still active — it has
killed Ben Gardner.

BB 51:20—53:24: People from Amity as well as out-of-town
visitors flock to the beach.

BB 53:24—56:47: People swim in the sea.

BB 56:47–57:33: A plastic shark fin causes panic among the swimmers.
BB 57:33–59:27: People race out of the water.
BB 59:27–61:28: The shark eats a man in the small bay – act climax.
BB 61:28–63:36: Brody and his family are at the hospital. The mayor signs a contract because Brody wants to hire Quint to kill the shark.
BB 63:36–66:21: Brody and Quint work out a deal for hunting the shark. Quint allows Hooper to join them.
BB 66:21–69:40: They prepare the boat.

Act 3: 69:40–108:20
BB 69:40–71:39: Brody, Hooper and Quint head to sea on Quint's boat. Brody spreads shark chum but does not enjoy it.
BB 71:39–73:29: Quint gets a fish on the line.
BB 73:29–75:30: The fish breaks off.
BB 75:30–76:50: Quint and Hooper argue.
BB 76:50–77:45: Quint wants Brody to keeping chumming for the shark.
BB 77:45–79:11: Brody spreads chum. The crew sees the shark for the first time.
BB 79:11–82:53: They hunt the killer shark.
BB 82:53–85:50: The trio enjoy the evening below deck.
BB 85:50–89:18: Quint tells his backstory why he hunts sharks.
BB 89:18–90:49: Brody, Hooper and Quint sing.
BB 90:49–92:28: The shark rams the boat.
BB 92:28–94:51: The boat's motor is damaged. Quint destroys the radio.
BB 94:51–97:51: They hunt the shark.

BB 97:51—99:09: Quint wants to pull in the barrels. They do so.

BB 99:09—102:50: The shark defends itself against the men hunting it.

BB 102:50—105:31: They draw the shark toward the beach. The boat's motor explodes — act climax.

BB 105:31—106:26: They want to poison the shark.

BB 106:26—108:20: Brody, Hooper and Quint put the shark cage together. Hooper prepares the poison harpoon. The crew lowers the cage into the water. They get Hooper ready to dive. Hooper climbs into the shark cage.

Act 4: 108:20—117:33

BB 108:20—110:06: Hooper tries to poison the shark but loses the poison harpoon.

BB 110:06—112:08: The shark destroys the cage. Hooper manages to escape from the cage and hides behind seaweed.

BB 112:08—114:03: The shark destroys the boat and eats Quint (*catastrophe*). Brody wants to kill the shark (PAC). He throws the gas bottle into its mouth (*preparation*).

BB 114:03—116:07: Brody shoots at the shark (CPAC), which explodes — resolution of the conflict.

BB 116:07—117:33: Brody and Hooper are happy the shark is dead. They swim back toward land.

Note

Pages 16—19 contain the story template I have developed. The template was also created with the help of my film analysis and provides structural elements for giving shape to screenplays. Of course, writers don't have to structure their script with four acts and eight sequences, as shown in the template. A film contains as many acts and sequences as it needs.

Story template

F: A FILM has a certain length: start—end. A film minute corresponds more or less to one page of a screenplay.

A: A film is divided into ACTS . . .

S: . . . and acts into SEQUENCES. Sequences are approx. 7 to 15 minutes in length.

U: Sequences are divided into UNITS (each about 4–5 minutes).

BB: Units are subdivided into BUILDING BLOCKS (each about 1–3 minutes).

M: Building blocks are subdivided into MICROS. A one-minute building block contains two micros, while a two-minute building block contains four. A three-minute building block consists of six micros. Duration of micros: from several seconds up to approx. fifty seconds.

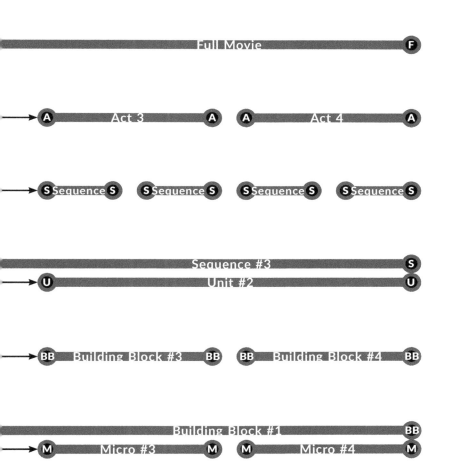

Jaws

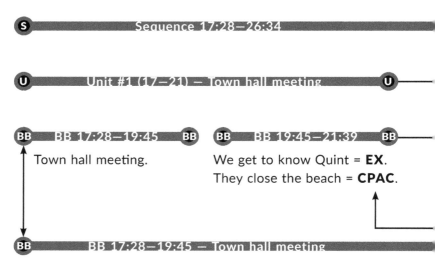

Sequence 17:28—26:34

Unit #1 (17—21) — Town hall meeting

BB 17:28—19:45

Town hall meeting.

BB 19:45—21:39

We get to know Quint = **EX**.
They close the beach = **CPAC**.

BB 17:28—19:45 — Town hall meeting

M 17:28—17:59

Mrs. Kintner wants someone to kill the shark = **PAC**.

M 17:59—18:31

Practice makes perfect: watch *Jaws* after reading the book and find the element or elements at work in this micro.

The story element system

A building block consists of one or more elements. An element may or may not drive the story forward. There are eleven types of elements:

— Exposition (**EX**)
— Catastrophe

Sequence 17:28—26:34 **S**

U **Unit #2 (21—26) — The hunt starts** **U**

BB **BB 21:39—23:31** **BB**

Brody reads books about sharks = **EX**.

BB **BB 23:31—26:34** **BB**

Two men fish for the shark = **CPAC**.

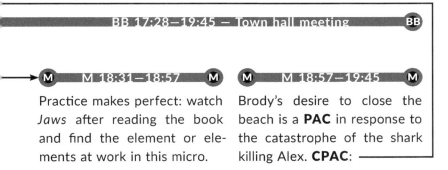

BB 17:28—19:45 — Town hall meeting **BB**

M **M 18:31—18:57** **M**

Practice makes perfect: watch *Jaws* after reading the book and find the element or elements at work in this micro.

M **M 18:57—19:45** **M**

Brody's desire to close the beach is a **PAC** in response to the catastrophe of the shark killing Alex. **CPAC**: ———

Note: there are four kinds of catastrophe (see page 24 1.2)
- Emotional reaction (**ER**)
- Plan against a catastrophe (**PAC**)
- Preparation (**PR**)
- Carrying out the plan against a catastrophe (**CPAC**)
- Philosophizing (**PH**)
- Story filler (**SF**)

A character crossing a street is a single action. If we categorize this single action as a CPAC or as any other element, this single action is more than just a single action — it is also a tool we can use to develop additional actions. The categorization of single actions gives us as-yet-unsuspected possibilities for creating stories. Chapter 1 presents the eleven categories/elements I've identified.

1

Story element system (SES)

- Exposition (EX)
- Four kinds of catastrophe
- Emotional reaction (ER)
- Plan against a catastrophe (PAC)
- Preparation (PR)
- Carrying out the plan against a catastrophe (CPAC)
- Philosophizing (PH)
- Story filler (SF)

STORY ELEMENT SYSTEM

1.1 Exposition (EX) — we get to know someone or something

Exposition introduces either a film character or the audience to something new, e.g. a person, a thing/situation/event etc. In *A Prayer for the Dying* (1987), mortician Jack Meehan prepares a woman's body. At the same time, he tells Martin Fallon the story of how the woman came to die. We can categorize this brief story relating the woman's death as *exposition* because the story presents both Martin and the audience with new information. This *exposition*, however, doesn't contain any information that is vital for an understanding of the film's central plot.

Let's look at a classic *exposition* scene from *Jaws*: in building block (BB) 04:55—06:49 (see page 11), we get to know Martin Brody, his wife Ellen, and their two sons Michael and Sean. We learn that they bought a house the previous year and that Martin works as police chief. We also discover from a dialogue that Amity has a very low crime rate. When Ellen asks Martin (who is about to drive to the beach to examine the discovery of human remains) to be careful, Martin hints in a few words at how insignificant the crime rate in Amity is.

Writers can build *exposition* into a building block that already contains another element or elements. The BB 04:55—06:49 introduces us to Brody and his family. This BB, however, does not restrict itself simply to *exposition*. A body has been found on the beach (*catastrophe*). Brody gets a call about it, which in turn triggers a PAC (*plan against a catastrophe*) in Brody: he wants to check the remains that have been discovered. This PAC drives the story forward to its next BB (BB 06:49—08:33) and element, a CPAC (*carrying out the plan against a catastrophe*): Brody drives to the beach and checks the body. This building block also contains a further element: *exposition* (for the audience). While Brody is driving to the beach, the audience gets to see various parts of Amity, and the following dialogue between Brody and Cassidy is also *exposition*.

More examples from Jaws
BB 26—29: we get to know Hooper.
BB 69—71: the gas bottle that kills the shark at the end of the movie is presented to the audience.

Midnight Run (1988)
BB 00:17—03:11: in this *exposition*, we meet Jack Walsh, who practices the risky profession of bounty hunter — Bouchet shoots at him. We are also introduced to Marvin Dorfler, another bounty hunter. In a dialogue between Walsh and Dorfler, we hear about a two-faced bail bondsman named Moscone: Moscone has simultaneously contracted both Walsh and Dorfler to arrest Bouchet, which puts Walsh and Dorfler into conflict. Walsh's line of work means that he's surrounded by scumbags who are either trying to kill him or set him up. But we also discover that Walsh is not the kind of guy to take these things lying down. When Dorfler unfairly seizes Bouchet for himself, Walsh doesn't hesitate to take Bouchet back: Walsh outsmarts Dorfler with a trick, a running gag throughout the film, and knocks him out. Jack is a quick-witted character with a boxer's talents.

Shaping your exposition
Screenwriters can focus their *exposition* and give us a lot of information in an expository scene to help us understand the film, as demonstrated in the road action comedy *Midnight Run* above.

Conversely, writers can also spread the information across several scenes to help the viewer understand the film, as demonstrated in the thriller *Jaws* above.

Concise exposition from my story SMKT

Klara goes into a supermarket. While she's trying to find the right teabags, she gets a call from her boyfriend Ben. He threatens a smooching ban for a month if she's late for dinner that night. Klara reassures him and promises that she'll be on time. In the background, supermarket employee Jürgen accidentally drops a packet of chocolate hearts on the floor, and they roll through the store. Klara finishes her call and asks Jürgen for help finding the teabags she needs. Felix holds up the supermarket and takes Klara hostage, despite Jürgen volunteering to be a hostage instead. Felix exchanges gunfire with the arriving cops. Felix shoots at Klara. Jürgen throws himself between them protectively and takes the bullet in his shoulder. What do we learn from this *exposition*? Klara loves tea, but also loves stick-in-the-mud Ben, who needs to be replaced by a real man (Jürgen). Also, Felix has financial problems.

1.2 Catastrophe

We differentiate between four kinds of catastrophe. The word *catastrophe* is applied in an unusual way in this book, being used to describe not only negative events, but positive ones, as well. This unusual usage makes working with the other elements simpler — I will clarify this with a few examples. This approach allows you to control your stories in a new way.

1. Negative event (negative catastrophe): the shark devours Alex

in *Jaws*.

2. Positive event (positive catastrophe): Solomon Vandy finds a diamond in *Blood Diamond*.

3. A character achieves his or her goal (positive catastrophe): Brody kills the shark in *Jaws*.

4. A character does not achieve his or her goal (negative catastrophe): Coetzee doesn't get the diamond in *Blood Diamond*.

1.3   Negative event (NE) — negative catastrophe

A negative event fills many roles. An NE, for example, can trigger an act or can help a character evolve in his internal conflict like Brody in . . .

Jaws

Act breakdown for *Jaws*: start—21—69—108—117. The shark, in the external conflict (e-story), kills a man in the small bay (see BB 59—61 on p. 13), triggering the third act. This *negative event* (NE), however, does more than just kick off the third act. It also fulfills an additional task, allowing Brody to develop in his internal conflict (i-story). Brody's internal conflict: he won't go into the water because he's afraid of water. After the shark kills the man in the small bay, Brody charges into the water and pulls his son back to dry land — his son was in the water when the shark killed the man. Without this shark attack, Brody would never have entered the water and would therefore never have evolved in his i-story. Paradoxically, the shark attack helps Brody overcome his fear of water, which gives credibility to Brody's venturing out on the ocean in the third act, when Brody, Quint and Hooper hunt the shark in open waters.

As Good as it Gets (1997)

Act breakdown: start—26—81—111—128. BB 61—64: Carol visits Melvin at home and tells him that she won't sleep with him (cf. shark kills man in the bay [BB 59—61]). For Melvin, this rejection is a *negative event*, to which he reacts: motivated by this NE, Melvin visits Simon in BB 64—66 and brings him soup (cf. after the shark attack, Brody charges into the water). Melvin takes care of Simon in this building block, and the two chat like old friends. Without this soup-and-chat scene, it would not be believable, from the third act, for Melvin to drive Simon to Baltimore in Frank's car (cf. from the third act, Brody lives on a boat out on the open sea). Why not believable? Because Simon hits Melvin in BB 56—58 and throws him out of the apartment. Apart from that, until we reach BB 64—66, there isn't a single scene in which Melvin personally takes care of any other person. The *negative event*, that Carol refuses to sleep with Melvin, does not initiate the third act, and is only necessary for Melvin's character development. Triggered by this *negative event*, Melvin's character undergoes a further development in BB 64—66 (he takes care of Simon [cf. Brody charges into the water]), lending credibility to Melvin's ongoing character development, starting in the third act.

1.4   Positive event (PE) — positive catastrophe

In BB 73—76 of *Enemy of the State* (1998), Dean receives the murder video from his son. Receiving the video, which is a *positive event* (because things then turn in Dean's favor), I categorize as a positive <u>catastrophe</u>, because the event triggers a PA<u>C</u>: after receiving the video, Dean wants to meet with Brill. This example demonstrates the utility of using the expression *catastrophe* for both negative and positive events – it facilitates working with the other elements, for example PACs and CPACs.

1.5 A character achieves his or her goal – positive catastrophe

In BB 41–43, Hooper cuts open the tiger shark. In BB 33–34, Hooper formulates his goal – he wants to cut open the tiger shark (PAC).
In BB 113–116 Brody kills the shark with an exploding gas bottle. In BB 61–63, Brody's goal – he wants to kill the shark (PAC) – becomes clear.

Why can we categorize *achieving a goal* as a positive and/or negative catastrophe? Whereas *achieving a goal* for character #1 represents a *positive event*, his achievement represents a *negative event* for character #2, who subsequently forms a PAC, a plan to counteract the negative catastrophe. An example:

Midnight Run
BB 91–93: Jack, the main character, loses The Duke to Dorfler. I subdivided this BB into two catastrophes (that is, one single action [Jack loses The Duke] can consist of several elements):
1. *A character achieves his goal* (positive catastrophe): Dorfler apprehends The Duke.
2. *Negative event* (negative catastrophe): Jack loses The Duke to Dorfler.

The event in BB 91–93 contains two different plot lines (Jack's and Dorfler's) that must be further developed separately. After Jack loses The Duke to Dorfler, Jack's plot line diverges from that of Dorfler, who wants to take The Duke to Serrano's men (PA<u>C</u>) after catching him (*a character achieves his goal* = positive <u>catastrophe</u>). But because the film continues for around thirty minutes after this <u>event</u>, I don't categorize this <u>event</u> as *a character does not achieve his goal* for Jack, but rather as *a negative event*.

1.6 A character does not achieve his or her goal – negative catastrophe

In BB 115–117 of *Enemy of the State*, Reynolds does not manage to get the murder video and dies in a hail of bullets.

1.7 Emotional reaction to an event (ER)

An *emotional reaction* is a response to an event. This can as easily include a funeral as a party. If a character in a film reacts to an event indifferently or sarcastically, this reaction also falls into the ER category.

In BB 34–36 of *Jaws*, Mrs. Kintner grieves for Alex and blames Brody for Alex's death. This ER scene is simultaneously a *negative event* for Brody, because Mrs. Kintner's ER makes him see his guilt in Alex's death – the shark killed Alex because Brody didn't close the beach. BB 34–36 thus contains two elements: for Mrs. Kintner, an *emotional reaction* that is, at the same time, a *negative event* for Brody that triggers an *emotional reaction* from him in the following BB (36–37): his guilt in Alex's death (NE) makes him depressed (ER).

Casablanca (1942)
24:17: Ilsa visits Rick's Café (*negative event* for Rick Blaine).
34:49: Rick Blaine falls into depression.

Kick-Ass (2010)
BB 27—30: Kick-Ass rescues a man (*positive event* [PE]) from three thugs who are beating him up (NE).
BB 30—32: society reacts positively (*emotional reaction*) to Kick-Ass and his heroics.

Defining characters
A character's emotional reactions define his or her nature and personality, which is why we perceive Rick Blaine as a sensitive guy and criminals generally as tough, hardened people. If a character experiences a range of emotions, then this variety of emotional reactions shapes him or her into a multidimensional character. An example from *Casablanca*: Rick plays the tough guy in one scene, then in a later scene falls into depression because of his ex-love Ilsa. Search your script for missing character reactions and use them to "stretch" your screenplay. The moviegoers won't notice if a story is "stretched" by characters' reactions, because moviegoers themselves experience emotions and it is not unfamiliar to them to feel joy or get angry or cry because their mother-in-law is about to visit. Expand film characters into "real" human beings and allow them to experience a range of emotional reactions. An example: by grieving for his recently deceased dog, a merciless mobster takes on an additional dimension, one that makes him more multifaceted and interesting. We may not feel any more sympathetic toward the mobster, but he will be more than just a bland accessory to push the story along. Because of his various emotions, he comes across as a "real" human being.

A character's reaction moves a story forward

The combination of an event and a character's reaction to that event drives a story forward. A fictional example to illustrate the point: Marie, Agnes, Linus and Alex are sitting at the kitchen table. They are engaged in a conversation that, for the audience, is boring. How do we add some oomph to this scene? With a CPAC: Agnes splits up with Linus, ending their relationship because *she doesn't feel loved* — for her, this is a *negative event*. Linus reacts with relief: "Finally!" Linus's reaction, also a *negative event* for Agnes, makes Agnes furious (ER). She accuses him of never having loved her. Linus responds with a shrug and suppresses a smile. Agnes boils over. She grabs Linus's phone and hurls it out the open window from the fifth floor. Marie, horrified, jumps to her feet, storms across to the window and peers out. However, she does so with so much energy that she falls out of the window. She lands in a tree, badly gashing her face on the branches. Agnes is deeply sorry and Marie is seriously hurt. Marie swallows a few painkillers and summarily throws Agnes out of the apartment. The pills give Marie hallucinations, which is why she wants to go to the hospital immediately. Her hallucinations make her believe that she will die if a doctor does not treat her wounds immediately. But there are two problems: Linus and Alex have drunk far too much to be able to drive, and a taxi is at least an hour away. So Marie goes out onto the balcony and calls down to the crying Agnes to come back and drive her to the hospital. The combination of an event and a character's reaction to that event drives the story forward. The audience appreciates change and development, and hates stagnation. Think of the pages of your script, regardless of genre, as a circus, and entertain your audience with clever conflict.

1.8   Plan (intention/idea) against a catastrophe (PAC)

A character wants to do something in response to a positive or negative catastrophe and subsequently develops a plan. A PAC often contains the word *want/wants*, implying a goal: Mrs. Kintner wants someone to kill the shark (BB 17–19).

Catastrophes and their corresponding PACs drive a story forward, regardless of genre. If a character does not actively pursue a goal, a story has trouble developing. In *SMKT*, Klara can't find a single teabag anywhere in her kitchen (NE). Without her PAC wanting to buy teabags in the supermarket Klara would stay at home. A PAC, until it is actually carried out, remains no more than an idea or a plan to do something special to counteract a catastrophe. Likewise, if Felix does not formulate a PAC of his own (to rob the supermarket), he would also stay at home and the viewer would write a commensurate review on IMDb. com: "Dull, tedious film." Without contradictory goals getting in each other's way, conflicts rarely arise. A lack of conflict/catastrophes is characteristic of low-suspense films – characters carry on meaningless conversations (*philosophizing* [PH]) and no one seems to know what they want. If characters don't pursue goals, a story does not develop at a suitable pace. If no questions are thrown up, viewers expect no answers. And if questions don't pull viewers to the edge of their seats, they get bored.

A PAC, logically, has to harmonize with the inner life/personality of the character that comes up with the PAC. After the shark kills the man in the small bay, Brody charges into the water. By going into the water, Brody manages to shake off part of his fear of water, making his PAC, his plan to finish off the killer shark out on the open sea, believable. Let's look at a fictional example to show how a character's personality can influence a PAC: good-natured, shy Hugo suffers from social anxiety disorder and has no friends. One day, Arthur robs Hugo right in front of his parents. Hugo's father is unable to help because his arms and legs are all in casts after he broke them blowing his nose. Hugo's mother calls the police, but forgets why she's calling and ends up ordering a pizza from them. Which PAC reflects Hugo's personality? First PAC: Hugo wants to simply drop the matter. With everything we know about him, this is the most believable PAC. Second PAC: Hugo wants to go to the police. This PAC is not credible, because Hugo knows for certain that, if he does, Arthur will take revenge on him. And because Hugo is shy, he wants to avoid another confrontation with a guy like Arthur. Third PAC: Hugo wants to talk things through with Arthur. This PAC, like #1, is also credible, but calls for a certain amount of courage. This in turns means Hugo has to get a little drunk to make the CPAC more believable. Fourth PAC: Hugo gets to know a nice group of people and, with their help, undergoes a change in his personality until he feels the desire to take revenge on Arthur. Hugo's CPAC might look like this: Hugo breaks into Arthur's apartment and plants drugs. Then he calls the police and gives them an anonymous tip-off. Because Arthur already has a criminal record, the police don't waste any time. They arrange a search warrant, find the drugs, and arrest Arthur. As he's being taken away, Hugo waves to him from the other side of the street.

Another example from Jaws

BB 102–105: the boat's engine explodes (*negative event*/negative catastrophe).

BB 105—106: the crew initiates a plan to poison the shark with strychnine (PAC).

The Matrix (1999)

BB 79—81: Agent Smith arrests Morpheus (NE), who has sacrificed himself for Neo.

BB 89—91: Tank wants to kill Morpheus before Morpheus reveals the codes to Smith. Tank's plan to kill Morpheus is a PAC in response to the *negative event* of Morpheus's arrest and the possibility that he might reveal the codes to Smith. The PAC to kill Morpheus, however, is simultaneously a *negative event/ negative catastrophe* for Morpheus's crew and this negative catastrophe calls for a PAC.

BB 91—93: to save Tank from having to kill Morpheus, Neo plans to free Morpheus instead (PAC).

1.9   Preparation (PR) — the CPAC must be prepared

Mrs. Kintner wants someone to kill the shark (PAC). Starting in the 27th minute, people from Amity and elsewhere prepare to hunt the shark (PR). Someone has a date? PR: he reads a book about etiquette. She buys some decent clothes.

Another example from Jaws

BB 105—106: the crew develops a plan to poison the shark with strychnine (PAC).

BB 106—108: the crew assembles the shark cage (PR) — see page 14.

The Matrix
BB 91—93: Neo wants to free Morpheus (PAC).
Micro 94:42—95:08: Trinity and Neo pick up some weapons (PR).

Enemy of the State
BB 33—36: Thomas Reynolds's men don't find the murder video on Robert Dean (NE).
BB 36—37: Reynolds wants to destroy Dean's life and credibility (PAC).
Unit 37—42: Reynolds's men bug Dean's house and clothing (PR).

The Rundown (2003)
BB 67—69: Beck discovers that Hatcher has captured the beautiful Mariana (NE).
BB 69—71: Beck and Travis want to free Mariana (PAC).

BB 71—73 (building block contains several elements): Beck wants to attack Hatcher's town (PAC): this PAC, for Hatcher, is a *negative event*. To counteract Beck's PAC, Hatcher wants a curfew for the town (PAC).
Micro 73:08—73:43: *preparation*: Hatcher's men drive the inhabitants out of the town and take up positions on the streets and rooftops. They chain Mariana and the rebels to a wooden house. Hatcher's men patrol the town.

1.10   Carrying out the plan against a catastrophe (CPAC)

PAC: Mrs. Kintner wants someone to kill the shark. CPAC: from minute 23, Denherder and Charlie set baits for the killer shark. From minute 26, both Amity locals and visitors want to kill the shark. Once they have made their *preparations*, they hunt the killer shark (CPAC), but kill a tiger shark instead — not the right shark at all. This is a *negative event* for which Hooper formulates a PAC: he wants to cut the tiger shark open. CPAC: from minute 41, Hooper cuts the tiger shark open. However, he finds no human remains inside it, proving that the killer shark is still out there, another *negative event* for which Hooper expresses a PAC: he wants to go out in his boat at night to find the real killer shark.

Another example from Jaws

BB 106:26—108:20: Brody, Hooper and Quint assemble the shark cage (PR).
BB 108:20—110:06: Hooper, underwater and armed with the poisoned harpoon, waits inside the cage for the shark (CPAC), wanting to kill it with poison (PAC).

Everything goes wrong = suspense

A CPAC that does not go according to plan generates suspense. A perfect example of this kind of storytelling can be found in *Back to the Future* (1985), when Doc Emmett Brown wants to send Marty McFly back to 1985: the DeLorean time machine makes several false starts. Doc Brown cuts the cable they need to conduct the energy from the lightning. After everything that could go wrong has gone wrong, Marty McFly and Doc Brown are able to achieve their goal at the last second, which causes a tremendous sense of relief in the viewer. Look at a scene in your script and think about what you can use from that scene (a suitcase, bicycle, car or pen, for example) to generate tension because the item or items in question don't do what they're supposed to.

1.11   Philosophizing (PH)

Characters debate or shed light on a point of fact, for example past events, or a theme, for example the meaning of life. Toward the end of *Pulp Fiction* (1994), Vincent and Jules discuss the consumption of pork and a divine miracle that has helped Jules to change his ways — he doesn't want to kill people anymore. In *A Prayer for the Dying*, Martin Fallon goes behind the pulpit in church and *philosophizes* with Michael Da Costa, the priest, about God and about how he, Martin, has destroyed himself with his behavior.

1.12   Story Filler (SF)

Story filler refers to actions you can delete without compromising the sense of the story. Occasional *story filler* does not damage a story and is an ideal means of unobtrusively extending a story — see page 96: *Using elements to stretch a story*.

Note
If you want to learn to write good exposition (or any other element), analyze how *exposition* is handled in some movies you like. Do so with every other element. Analyze! Analyze! Analyze!

If you want to know anything about screenwriting . . . don't analyze guidebooks, analyze movies. You want to know how to write good dialogues? Read comic books and analyze 89 movies, not 89 how-to books.

The End of Chapter One

If every story is made up of elements, why not simply break the single actions of a story down into one or another of the eleven elements at the development stage, or consciously create and deliberately use elements to create a story?

2

Every person has an imagination that he or she can stimulate — for example, with the story element system, which can absolutely be used as a creative technique to develop scenes for a story.

CONNECT TECHNIQUE

2.1   Using elements to expand on an initial situation

We create an initial situation, then develop several elements we can use to craft a brief story from this initial situation.

Initial situation

NE: Olav races onto the platform in time to see his double-decker train departing. He's going to be late for work, which is why he swears out loud (ER). For his ex-wife, his late arrival at work means that she has *achieved her goal* — she was the one who orchestrated his crisis by slashing the tires on his car (CPAC for her, NE for him).

Develop a subsequent element

To develop further elements, we use the elements to ask ourselves a few questions about the initial situation. The aim is to use the answers to create scenes for our story.

For whom is Olav's swearing a *negative event*? A homeless guy, sleeping on a bench on the platform, is woken by Olav's cursing.

What would be a believable CPAC for the missed train? Olav calls his boss to tell him he'll be late. We soon realize, however, that this call is a CPAC little entertainment value and can be scrubbed. Why doesn't Olav take a taxi to work? Because of the traffic jams gridlocking the city (NE).

What *negative event* can we attach to being late? Let's take a closer look at Olav's boss. Would it make much sense to create a boss with no entertainment value? No! So getting to work late means getting in trouble with a quick-tempered boss. CPAC:

Olav calls him and tells him he's been mugged. *Preparation*: Olav tears several buttons off his shirt, rubs dirt on it, and messes up his hair. Then he smiles at the homeless guy and tells him that he has to look like a mugging victim for his idiot boss.

What *negative event* can we add to make Olav's situation even worse and ensure a payoff that entertains viewers? In the city, Olav and his boss — now in a good mood — run into the homeless guy, who asks Olav: "Hey, aren't you that guy who ripped his shirt and rubbed dirt on it so he could make his idiot boss think he got mugged?" And because the boss is so hot-tempered, he has a corresponding ER to this NE, right there in the middle of the busy city.

Develop different versions of elements

In expanding on an initial situation or developing it in an unexpected direction, we can create, for example, several *emotional reactions* to a *negative event* and can perhaps connect these ER's together. For example: after missing his train, Olav bashes the homeless guy with his briefcase or bursts out in a full-throated Beethoven aria. Maybe Olav is so angry that he smokes three cigarettes at once. Let's assume that Olav, responding emotionally, beats the homeless guy with his briefcase while listening to Beethoven. We categorize this scene for the homeless man and a passerby as a *negative event*. What element can we append to this *negative event*? An ER: the passerby is horrified by Olav's behavior. Which ER do we give the homeless man as a result of the beating? Perhaps an unconventional ER: the homeless man just laughs at Olav and pokes fun at him: "Hey man, stop hitting me with your leather case! I'm a vegetarian, if only for financial reasons. Or maybe you've got a meatball in there? For mercy's sake I hope it's between two slices of bread." Then a CPAC: the passerby steps in to help the homeless guy. Olav and the passerby struggle, and the passerby falls onto the tracks (NE) just as the train is arriving. And just like that, we've worked out a scene that will keep viewers entertained.

Which elements can we apply to the initial situation, the homeless man is lying on the bench on the platform? The man could be dead (NE). Or he could be an undercover investigator watching four suspicious-looking people (CPAC) who are dealing drugs and want to sell to Olav (PAC). The more elements we apply to a situation, the more ideas we develop to which we can apply additional elements, thus developing more scenes for our story.

Olav boards the next double-decker train
To work out Olav's commute on the train, I will use the story element system and mark some of the developed actions with the corresponding elements.

Olav wants to buy a ticket
Olav goes to the ticket inspector (CPAC) because he wants to buy a ticket (PAC), but he realizes he does not have his wallet on him (NE). Then he looks out the window of the already moving train and sees the homeless guy waving Olav goodbye with a handful of banknotes and Olav's credit card (NE). Why do I use the CPAC *Olav goes to the ticket inspector to buy a ticket?* Because it makes sense and offers material for more scenes.

Olav has no money for a ticket
Seeing the ticket inspector, who is accompanied by two cops with two unmuzzled police dogs and is checking tickets (NE for

Olav), Olav makes a run for it in the opposite direction (CPAC). Olav hides from the ticket inspector, and at some point actually climbs out onto the roof of the train, followed by one of the cops with his German shepherd, who finally apprehends Olav and arrests him (NE for Olav, *goal achieved* for the cops). Why do I use the *negative event* of Olav having no money for a train ticket? My thought process goes like this: how do I make Olav's situation worse? With a ticket inspector. How can I tighten the screws even more? With cops and German shepherds. Have you ever seen two German shepherds used when a ticket inspector checks tickets, or a German shepherd on the roof of a train? Unrealistic, but plausible. No denial: allow every image, every thought that comes to mind!

The cops haul Olav away to the police station

For Olav, this CPAC for the officers represents a *negative event*. In this sequence, the cops are not friendly toward Olav and refuse to let him make a phone call. Because the cop on the train had to climb out onto the roof, he makes sure Olav's stay at the station is particularly unpleasant by making him clean the toilets. Then the cop escorts Olav to a bank (CPAC), where Olav calls a friend and is able to obtain cash to pay his fine (*goal achieved*). If Olav hadn't climbed out onto the train roof, the cops would have simply taken his details and let him go. But how much entertainment value would that have for viewers who are able to whip out their phone faster than Clint Eastwood can draw his gun in *A Fistful of Dollars* and write a scathing review on IMDb.com?

Two men rob the bank

The cop leaves the bank. When Olav is also ready to leave, two bad guys stage a holdup at the bank (NE). To find an event that complicates Olav's life while he's inside the bank, I ask myself this question: what *positive* or *negative event* or ER of a bank customer would make Olav's life harder? Maybe a bank robbery? A blocked toilet? A crying customer? An explosion in the vault? The explosion causes the bank doors to lock automatically and Olav, suspected of having detonated the bomb, can't get out.

Work out the train sequence

To work out the train sequence in detail, I use the *Olav and the cop on the train roof* scene for the sequence finale and develop the scenes leading up to this. Olav boards the train and realizes that he's lost his money and his credit card. Another *negative event*: his phone chooses that moment to die, preventing him from buying a ticket with his phone, which is becoming more and more common these days. Logical CPAC: he scurries off in the opposite direction from the ticket inspector until he reaches the second-to-last passenger compartment. But where does the story go from here? Because no new actions occurred to me after this CPAC, I pushed myself to develop three ER scenes. Before that, however, I asked and answered one question for myself: who is in the train? Pensioners, commuters, families, a cat in a pet carrier, Mike Tyson, etc.

(Always look around and see what there is in a scene or location. In a train, we see not only people, but also objects, for example seats, suitcases, bicycles, a washing machine etc. Apply each element from the story element system in different versions to each person and object, and pose questions: what *negative event*, *positive event* (and all the other elements) could, for example, happen with a suitcase . . . or a person? A suitcase falls from the overhead rack . . . straight onto Olav's head. He's knocked unconscious and stays that way until the next station, so he doesn't need a ticket at all. What do we find, for example, inside a suitcase? Clothes? Drugs? Then apply different elements to the suitcase. *Negative event* for the owner, *positive event* for a plainclothes cop: the suitcase springs open. What do we see, for example, at a funeral (ER)? Mourners, a coffin, a priest, and all the rest. Then apply different elements to the mourners or the coffin — different ER scenes or *negative events*, for example. A mourner laughs out loud or has a heart attack. A worm squirms out of a hole, revolting a mourner, who reacts with disgust.)

Three ER scenes I have developed for the train sequence

1. A retiree couple are arguing.
2. A mother holds a crying child.
3. Kári, a cook on a submarine, stands in the aisle, angry at Olav.

Now we ask ourselves what *negative events* trigger these ER scenes. And please, keep at it! Tenacity is called for when you're trying to find the right events!

Negative events that trigger the ER scenes

In his haste, Olav accidentally bumps the child with his briefcase. He apologizes to the family, but the mother accuses Olav of deliberately injuring her child. A question arises: what do the arguing retirees have to do with this? Nothing! So I shift their conflict to the child's mother and father. The mother growls at her husband about his phone addiction, because of which he doesn't stick up for his family. Their escalating quarrel draws the attention of the ticket inspector and the police. But because their fight has little to do with Olav, I scrap it. I draft a fourth ER scene: a nun from an Icelandic order snaps at Olav because he made the child cry. The heated discussion between Olav and the nun makes several passengers think that Olav deliberately injured the child with his briefcase just for the fun of it. For the passengers, this is a *negative event*. And it makes one of them — a paralegal named Sigrún — furious (ER).

Develop a PAC to a negative event

Sigrún develops a PAC: she wants the ticket inspector to get involved and marches off to find him (CPAC). She spots him two compartments away. He is harassing a nice passenger for producing an invalid ticket and being too broke to buy another one. Sigrún tells the ticket inspector about Olav. How does the ticket inspector react emotionally to Sigrún? And why does he react the way he does? Here are three *emotional reactions* for the ticket inspector:

Three ER scenes

1. The ticket inspector snaps at Sigrún because he doesn't want to be interrupted while he's working.
2. He rejoices — he hates kids.
3. Because he despises people who beat kids, he loses his cool and flies into a rage. He develops a PAC: he wants to make Olav pay for hurting the child.

Prepare the CPAC (PR)

The ticket inspector orders the two policemen to stir up their dogs. The cops follow his orders. The German shepherds growl.

The situation is getting out of control

In Olav's compartment, the discussion is escalating to the point where several passengers want to attack Olav (PAC for the passengers, NE for Olav). For his part, Olav finds the entire situation absurd. All he wants to do is leave (PAC). He stalks away (CPAC), accidentally bumping into submarine cook Kári (NE), who is listening to *Highway to Hell* through headphones and lifting his bag down from the overhead storage. Olav apologizes, but Kári shouts angrily at him (ER). When the nun jumps to her feet and shouts at Kári that Olav beats children for fun, Olav realizes that it's time to run. He hurries up the eight steps to the upper-level of the carriage. Arriving in the upper compartment, Olav hears shouts of "Get him!" from the enraged crowd below. Looking back at the steps, he sees the irate mob charging upstairs, led by the nun. With the mob hot on his heels, Olav hurries down the steps at the other end of the compartment only to see Sigrún, the ticket inspector, and the two cops with their barking dogs. When Sigrún screams that Olav is the child-beater, one of the officers releases his dog, which races at Olav like an insane machine of muscle and bared teeth. Olav throws his briefcase at the dog. Mr. Jökull — that's the dog's name — catches the briefcase in midair while Olav, bathed in fearful sweat, ducks into the restroom and locks the door. He jumps up onto the toilet and kicks the window out of its frame. As if blown open by an explosion, the door is torn off its hinges, and the angry mob surges into the restroom. Olav, horrified, climbs out the window and onto the roof of the train. One of the maniacs below manages to grab his foot, but Olav kicks free. He runs along the train roof before he suddenly stops in his tracks: he has a very bad feeling. When he turns around, he sees Mike Tyson holding the snarling Mr. Jökull on the roof of the train, ready for the final showdown. Mike releases the dog, who chases the fleeing Olav. Olav, the dog, and Mike do battle. For this fight, I make myself develop three *negative events* — each fighter gets a *negative event* of their own, which gives structure to the fight.

Three negative events
Negative event for Olav: Mike overpowers him.
Negative event for Mike: Olav defeats him — WHAT?!
Negative event for the dog: the dog slips off the train roof. Olav manages to grab the dog at the last second and Mike hurries to help him. We use the last *negative event* for the climax.

The battle
Mike catches up with the fleeing Olav and knocks him down. In the fight, Mike uses pepper spray, normally only to be used against out-of-control dogs. Because of his badly swelling eyes, Olav goes into a rage (ER). His rage gives him superpowers — he defeats Mike and jumps across to the roof of the next train car. The dog chases him, but loses its footing and slips off the roof. Olav grabs the dog firmly by its paw and Mike hurries to help him. After this climax, the police arrest Olav and lead him away in handcuffs — the resolution of the sequence. Mike refuses to give the dog back to the officer. Sir Tyson loves his new friend.

Practice makes perfect
Develop three PACs that counteract the *negative event* of Olav not having a train ticket.

2.2   Developing ideas by making associations

Initially, the most important factor when making associations is less the quality of ideas and far more that you are putting your subconscious mind to work. Writers carry on a conscious dialogue with their subconscious mind — every writer's most vital tool.

Latent inhibition

To avoid being overwhelmed by stimuli, the brain possesses a filter function: latent inhibition. This function effectively filters out things that are unimportant. If the filter is too permeable, the brain will be flooded with stimuli and becomes delusional. In schizophrenia, the latent inhibition is reduced or even absent, which is why schizophrenic patients often suffer from a deluge of thoughts that they are unable to channel — as, for example, an exceptionally creative writer who utilizes his or her innumerable associations/ideas to create a story. Highly creative authors, like patients at risk for schizophrenia, often have a genetic variant of the Neuregulin 1 gene (look up "psychoticism creativity"). People with this variant are not only more susceptible to schizophrenia, but also more creative. And because latent inhibition is diminished in highly creative people, they also associate more profoundly — their brains think in a less filtered way. A synonym for association is connection, and connecting two or more ideas or thoughts leads to more ideas. A synonym for creativity is productivity. Productivity is the only point of differentiation between highly creative writers and less creative writers, who are nevertheless able to generate ideas by . . .

Increasing productivity with technique

Every human being is able to practice association. Some more, some less. Most people associate *monkey* with *banana*. Few, however, will associate *monkey* with *raise human child in the jungle* and then go on to develop the Tarzan story. The quality of associations is one factor, but is not the pivotal driver.

Less-outstanding ideas, structured in an exemplary way, also reach audiences. And while structuring ideas is not particularly complicated, producing usable ideas is another matter. But how do writers come up with usable ideas if they can't make claims to exceptional creativity? With tenacity, research, and the story element system (SES), which supports the search for ideas that can be turned into stories.

We'll look at a simple example: let's think about the elements that can occur in a **car repair shop** (Idea 1). First, we create a mind map: what do we find in a repair shop? Among other things, a car lift. **Negative event** (Idea 2): a vehicle falls off the car lift and is damaged. Now we ask ourselves what the result of this connection is supposed to be: Idea 1 + Idea 2 = ? To be able to answer this question, we first answer the following one: if Jack (Idea 1) beats his dog (Idea 2), how does the dog generally respond? It whines and whimpers = Idea 3/result of the connection. **ER**: Hans, who runs the repair shop, is angry = Idea 3/result of the connection. Now we change the emotions in the ER scene: Hans isn't angry after all, but instead sad or nervous. Why nervous? Who owns the car, and why would that make Hans nervous? Or we swap the *emotional reaction* (ER) element for the *philosophizing* (PH) element, and have Hans react philosophically to the *negative event* — Hans is not angry but instead philosophizes with his employee about gravity and the power of a pay cut. What does this element (PH), which fulfills the same purpose as an ER, reveal about Hans's character? Or we change the *negative event* (car falls off car lift) to an ER scene: Hans kicks at the car lift angrily, causing the car to fall off. But what made Hans so furious in the first place?

We develop three *negative events*, one of which triggered Hans's *emotional reaction* (kicking the car lift in anger):
Negative event: it's going to rain the next day — but Hans wanted to play golf.
Negative event: Hans's favorite burger restaurant (Big Kahuna Burger) just went bankrupt.
Negative event: Hans, yet again, won nothing in the latest lottery draw.

New connection: **NE** (car falls off the car lift) + **ER** (nervous) = **?** If our unconscious doesn't offer us a third idea, we don't let it get to us. When I look up the term *nervous*, I find the synonym *fear*. New connection: **NE** (damaged car) + **ER** (fear) = **?** What causes Hans's fear? Let's make ourselves apply a few different elements to this connection. Which elements would make sense for this NE? PAC/CPAC. To work out a corresponding PAC, we need to know the car's owner, which we can find through questions and answers: what kind of person could make Hans so afraid? Maybe a Mafia godfather? But why would Hans be nervous? He could simply restore his inner equilibrium by repairing the car. The decisive factor in this particular case is time — the car is supposed to be handed back to the owner today. The godfather needs the car for his daughter's wedding. Solution: **NE + ER = PAC** (Hans wants to call the godfather). To use the SES effectively, writers need to ask and answer the right questions.

Let's assume for a moment that a writer has limited associative powers and is unable to form any associations at all with *car repair shop*, and instead we enlist Google to help us put together a mind map. What do we find in an auto repair shop?
Repair shop ⟶ car lift ⟶ bolts

A car lift doesn't just tip over by itself. Which means someone sabotaged it by loosening the bolts — I categorize this scene as a CPAC. But who doctored the bolts and why? To find the answer, we need to ask more questions: why is someone looking for revenge? To answer this, I'll turn to Google, in particular to show how a writer with average associative skills can still produce decent material for a story. People seek revenge because of unjust treatment or being deceived. With Google's help, we assemble a short mind map for deceived: cheating, theft, adultery. And now we turn to the question of what *negative event* could have preceded the CPAC of loosening the bolts? I create a mind map with the words cheating, theft, deceit:

1. NE: a poker player finds out about Hans cheating at their last poker night.
2. NE: Hans fires an employee for theft.
3. NE: Hans is having an affair with an employee's wife.

Why does Hans cheat at poker? Poker mind map: win money. Why does Hans need money so much that he cheats at poker? What *negative event* is Hans trying to counteract with the money? Let's take a straightforward example: Hans's wife is seriously ill and he needs the money to buy medicine — illegally, from abroad — that is not approved in Germany. Without much effort we create building blocks and a sequence with the ideas we have worked out above, if we continue to develop the story with the story element system in a comprehensible way:

Find an
| NE | 1.CPAC | 2.CPAC | 3.CPAC | 4.CPAC | NE/EX | ER | ? |
element.

NE: Hans's wife, Gundula, collapses at the breakfast table.

1. CPAC: Hans administers first aid. His PAC, obvious from the context, is that he wants to administer first aid. There is no need for him to put this into words.

2. CPAC: he calls an ambulance.

3. CPAC: the ambulance ferries Gundula to hospital.

4. CPAC: doctors examine Gundula in hospital while Hans calls his repair shop and tells an employee he's going to be in late.

NE/EX: Hans learns from a doctor that Gundula's inflammation levels are too high.

ER: Hans consoles Gundula, who is lying in a hospital bed.

If Hans finds himself in another country to buy the medicine his wife needs, we think about what kind of *negative events* might complicate things for him. He doesn't speak the local language and, as a result, falls into the hands of crooks. With the help of these two *negative events*, we tell a brief story: *positive event*/positive catastrophe for the crooks: they spot Hans in a shopping street, where he is asking a passerby in broken English about a certain building. PAC: the crooks plan to lure Hans into a trap and rob him. CPAC: they ambush him and rob him (*goal achieved* for the crooks, *negative event* for Hans). Trying to flee, Hans falls, knocks himself out, and subsequently suffers from amnesia. Because his ID has been stolen, no one knows who he is . . . meanwhile, his wife recovers and marries another man, because Hans has not reappeared and is now making a living in England as a test-sitter for couches and by putting the little stickers on apples.

2.3   The SES steering wheel

We can compare the story element system to a steering wheel that guides us unerringly through the storm of our unimaginativeness, if we are suffering from that.

A reminder
— Exposition (EX)
— Four kinds of catastrophe
    1. Something negative happens (NE).
    2. Something positive happens (PE).
    3. A character achieves his or her goal.
    4. A character does not achieve his or her goal.
— Emotional reaction (ER)
— Plan against a catastrophe (PAC)
— Preparation (PR)
— Carrying out the plan against a catastrophe (CPAC)
— Philosophizing (PH)
— Story filler (SF)

An example
To the single action *Diego jumps from the balcony* we apply each element using the SES steering wheel:

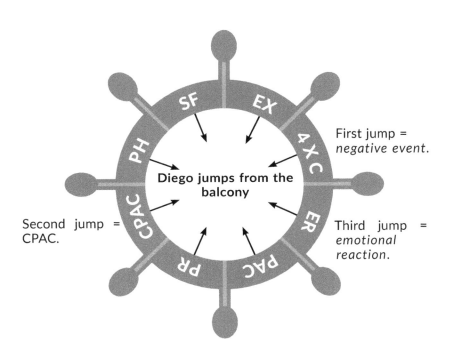

First jump = *negative event.*

Second jump = CPAC.

Third jump = *emotional reaction.*

We can categorize Diego's first jump from the balcony as a *negative event*, his second jump as a CPAC, his third jump as an ER, his fourth as *goal achieved*, etc. Of course, his jump can also cover several elements simultaneously. With the SES, we look at a single action from different perspectives, which leads to the creation of new actions. Play with ideas, and use the SES to generate new ones.

For our example with Diego above, we categorize his jump from the balcony as an *emotional reaction* and sketch three *negative events* connected to it, one of which triggered the *emotional reaction*, Diego's jump:

Negative event: Alma dumps Diego.
Negative event: Diego's goldfish died.
Negative event: There's no beer in the fridge.

Now we put the scene *Alma dumps Diego* (*negative event* for Diego, CPAC for Alma) into the SES steering wheel and apply each of the other elements to this scene, too:

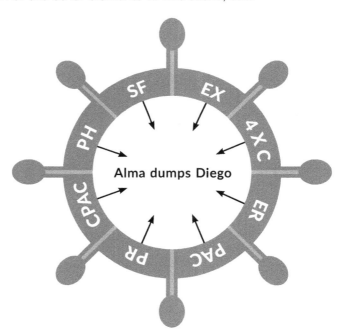

For Alma, we categorize her ending of their relationship in the first example as an ER, in the second example as a CPAC, etc. If we use the ER element, we use it to ask a question: why does Alma take out her anger (ER) on Diego? Alma is upset at Diego's mother, Mia, and wants revenge. Alma *achieves her goal* of taking revenge on Mia, because by separating from Diego she sends him into a fit of depression (ER), which is simultaneously a *negative event* for Mia. Alma's separation from Diego consists, for her, of two elements (ER + CPAC). ER: Alma vents her fury at Mia by ending her relationship with Diego. CPAC: with the CPAC (ending the relationship with Diego), Alma wants to achieve her goal of taking revenge on Mia.

Now we ask ourselves: for whom does the ER scene *Diego jumps off the balcony* represent a *negative event*? For Mia. PAC: Mia wants to comfort Diego. CPAC: she bakes him an apple pie. *Negative event*: the apple pie burns beyond redemption because Mia falls asleep in front of the TV. ER: feeling miserable about the burned pie, Mia jumps off the balcony. Fortunately, they only live on the first floor.

Note
When practicing with the SES, you may discover that, with the various scenes that evolve, you develop an idea for a story. The technique as applied just above, for example, inspired me to develop one: Alma and Mia wage their personal war, each using Diego as a kind of proxy and treating him horribly in the process, just so the two women can get their own back on each other. Alma, of course, wants Diego back, but Mia has already hooked him up with a gorgeous woman from Colombia.

Now the *Alma dumps Diego* scene is not an ER for Alma, but a CPAC in response to the *negative event* of Diego seeing another woman. Using the SES, we start by developing the story further in a way that makes sense: suspicious, Alma follows Diego secretly and finds out about his new girlfriend, a Swedish woman. We

devise a classical ER to this *negative event*: Alma cries her eyes out to a girlfriend. Next, however, we develop an unconventional ER: Alma is angry not only at Diego but also, because of him, at the Heavenly Father. So, she paints a church in different colours and sticks ten thousand marshmallow hearts to the outside of the church. We insert this second ER scene into the SES steering wheel and apply the different elements to it:

Let's look at the things likely to be near a church. *Negative event*: Alma is caught by the priest . . . or a member of the congregation stops Alma from doing what she's doing. Could this devout Christian be her future boyfriend? Now, with the help of Google, you can develop a mind map around the topic

Destruction of other people's property and apply the SES steering wheel to the results of your research to create a story.

2.4 Combining your scenes into a story

Once we've developed several scenes with the SES, the next step is to organize these scenes into a functioning story. Individual scenes have to be put into a sequence that relates them to each other – the thread of the story – otherwise the individual scenes remain individual scenes, no more, with no relation to the others. Let's take, for example, the scenes I've developed with the SES: the train scene, car repair shop, Mafia godfather, sick wife, hospital, medicine, poker, Hans robbed abroad, Diego jumps off the balcony. From these scenes, I can construct a story. It won't win an Oscar, of course, but it is intended to show how we can take the individual scenes we've developed with the SES – some of which have no relation to the others at all – and fashion a story:

We get to know Hans, who is in his repair shop working on the Mafia godfather's car for the mafioso's daughter's wedding. Hans discovers that his wife is seriously ill and that she needs expensive medicine that is not available in Germany because it is not approved. But because Hans is in debt and the bank won't give him a loan, he cheats at poker. He wins, but unfortunately for Hans, his deception is discovered and the other players pay him a visit in his apartment. He tries to escape by jumping off the balcony. But the players still catch him and take back the money he won. In financial dire straits, Hans turns instead to the Mafia boss and asks him for a loan, but again gets turned down. Instead, the boss wants to buy Hans's car, a 67 Mustang fastback, which was a wedding present from Hans's deceased father-in-law. When the godfather picks up the Mustang from Hans's repair shop, he is with his daughter and her future husband, who look adoringly at their wedding car, still being worked on in the shop. Hans takes a train to another country to buy the medicine for his wife. When he arrives, he is ambushed and robbed by crooks.

2.5 Connecting the SES with a mind map

To outline the path of my thoughts, I number the mind map in the sequence in which I developed the various scenes.

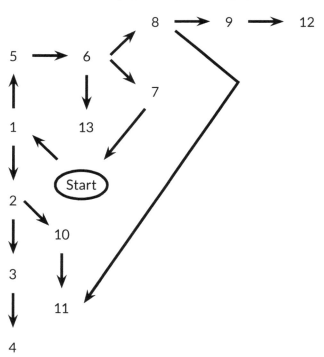

Start: Máté voluntarily commits himself to a psychiatric facility. (Nóra and Péter *achieve their goal*).

1: *Achieving a goal* precedes a CPAC, because a CPAC contains a goal that needs to be achieved. Why would someone want Máté in a state of despair (PAC)?

2: PAC: Péter wants to get even with Máté. But why? What *negative event* did Máté cause? And what exactly is Péter planning against Máté?

3: If we find the *negative event* that started everything, then we'll also find a PAC/CPAC.

4: NE: Máté has been physically abusing Nóra, his wife.

5: The final result of Nóra's and Péter's CPAC must be a *negative event* for Máté; he would not otherwise have committed himself to a psychiatric facility.

6: CPAC: Nóra and Péter secretly record Máté beating Nóra and post the video online. For Máté, the video represents a *negative event*, while for Nóra and Péter it represents a*chieving one of their goals*/positive catastrophe.

7: Because of the video, which goes viral, Máté loses his job. Friends and neighbors shun him. He gets death threats.

8: Nóra and Péter consider where to set up the camera in the apartment. When they find a hiding place for it, I categorize this as the element *goal achieved* (positive catastrophe). The two then develop PAC #B to supplement the element *goal achieved*: they want to lure Máté out of the apartment so they can actually hide the camera inside.

9: CPAC #B: Dániel, a friend of Nóra's, lures Máté to the pub to give Nóra and Péter a chance to hide the camera in the apartment. We can also *prepare* CPAC #B and develop it with additional elements (NE, PAC, CPAC, ER, etc.) into a 5-minute unit (see pages 16–19 about units). As an ER, I see an image of an anxious Nóra, frightened because, while involved in CPAC #B (luring her husband out of their home), he almost discovers her while she is hiding behind a car.

10: NE: Nóra and Péter have no clue what they can do against Máté. They think about what they can do against Máté.

11: PAC: Péter wants to video Máté the next time he attacks Nóra and post the video online. What does Péter's plan (PAC) to publicly humiliate Máté say about Péter's character? Why doesn't he take some other kind of action?

12: *Goal achieved*: Dániel and Máté drink a beer in the pub. What elements could we use to boost the tension? NE: Máté has forgotten something at home and wants to go and get it (PAC for Máté, NE for Dániel). What does Dániel's PAC in response to this *negative event* look like? Now it's your turn: come up with three PACs that counteract the *negative event*.

13. Máté learns about the as yet unreleased video (NE) and wants to get his hands on it (PAC) — another storyline with many conflicts to keep viewers entertained.

Note
Thinking in elements is an effective way of developing a story.

Quotes
"Never underestimate the power of thought; it is the greatest path to discovery." *Idowu Koyenikan, Wealth for All: Living a Life of Success at the Edge of Your Ability*

"A thought cannot awaken without awakening others." *Marie von Ebner-Eschenbach*

What do these quotes mean? They mean that screenwriters, through the mental effort they put in — with the help of the story element system, for example, which functions as an idea-creating tool — are rewarded with ideas they can use for their stories and screenplays.

Very important advice
Do not use the first element that comes to mind! Dig deeper! It's fun to play with ideas!

The End of Chapter Two

Analyze some films and ask yourself why the screenwriters used this or that element in structuring their story.

3

A story consists of elements that writers are able to arrange in various sequences to generate, for example, suspense, boredom, or a surprise moment. A synonym for arrange is structure.

STRUCTURING STORIES

3.1 Structuring a story with elements

Let's return to the story in Chapter 2 where Hans goes abroad to buy medicine but instead gets robbed.

Exposition
We get to know Hans, who is in his repair shop working on the Mafia godfather's car for his daughter's wedding.

Exposition
Hans discovers that his wife, Gundula, is seriously ill and that she needs expensive medicine that is not approved in good old Germany. For Hans, this *exposition* is also a *negative event*. If Hans hated his wife, however, this *exposition* would be a *positive event*.

Negative event
Hans is in debt and his bank won't grant him a loan, so he can't afford the expensive medication.

Goal achieved (Hans gets the money for the medicine)
After Hans sells his 67 Mustang to the godfather, we think about what elements we could use to continue to structure the story. Perhaps an ER:

Emotional reaction
Hans visits Gundula in hospital and tells her that he has the money for the necessary medicine. The couple then lie tearfully in each other's arms. For Gundula, this scene is also an *exposition* and a *positive event*, because this is when she finds out about Hans obtaining the money.

An ER can't hurt the story at this point, nor does it detract from the suspense. Properly structuring a story means using the right elements at the right points to keep the viewer engaged. Now, to return a little momentum to the story's structure, we should use elements that are more intense — the elements in a story should become more and more exciting: because the country he's going to can be dangerous, Hans wants to buy a pistol. In Germany, however, you can't legally buy a pistol without a firearms license. Hans doesn't want to get a pistol through the godfather — he believes it would be too risky. For our next element, we'll use the purchase of the gun from the introduction to this book — see page 9.

Preparation
Hans buys a gun illegally at the train station. We add an NE for Hans to the transaction: the police observe the deal, but Hans is able to escape them. This *preparation*, of course, is also a CPAC in response to the NE of Hans potentially getting into trouble when he goes abroad. To minimize the risk of being caught by customs officials at the border, Hans decides to travel by train.

Preparation
To avoid attracting unwanted attention, Hans puts on his best suit, combs his hair, and puts on glasses — he could be mistaken for an upstanding businessman.

Negative event
On the train, as it turns out, Hans does get targeted by customs officials — we want to keep the audience entertained, after all. When the officials search him, however, they don't find the revolver. Hans hid it in the restroom beforehand.

3.2 American Pit Bull – Act 1 (start–36)

Using my story *American Pit Bull* as an example, I'm going to demonstrate how I use elements in structuring a first act. Note: when crafting a story, I don't suppress or deny any thoughts, images, or emotions, nor do I reject them as unfit. Similarly, I don't attach any importance to reality, only to credibility.

Logline
Elderly Anna lives in Los Angeles and suffers from a fear of dogs, but with the help of an old abandoned pit bull used for illegal dogfighting years before, she ends the reign of a street gang that's been terrorizing her for years.

Exposition
A street gang regularly harasses Anna. But her complaints to the police go nowhere.

Emotional reaction
The next time she visits her dead husband's grave (his name was Jack), she complains to him about her misery and sheds tears about her unsolvable problem.

A character achieves her goal
Anna has a dream in which she is riding a wild lion and drives the street thugs into exile. Why do I categorize this dream as *a character achieves her goal*? Because Anna, through her dream, comes to understand that she needs a dog — a very large dog — to help her in her struggle with the gang. We find out in the next scene that the lion represents a dog:

Exposition
Anna meets with a friend and tells her about her dream and her plan to get herself a dog. Her friend welcomes the idea, but remarks on Anna's fear of dogs as a reason for her to buy a small dog instead.

PAC
Anna wants to get a huge dog — a pit bull.

Preparation
Anna buys books about pit bulls and studies them. She talks with her neighbor, Roman, who owns a teacup terrier — this scene demonstrates Anna's fear of dogs. But in time, Anna learns something about how to handle them.

CPAC
Anna and her friend visit an animal shelter to look at a pit bull. On their way to the kennel, the keeper tells Anna about the pit bull's history in illegal dog fighting, but that he nevertheless is a trustworthy dog.

Negative event
When Anna is standing in front of the kennel and the scarred pit bull creeps out of his dog house, Anna's fear overcomes her and she abandons her plan. The dog looks like a dragon that has fought a thousand battles.

ER
Heading home again, Anna complains to her friend about her fear of dogs.

PAC

Her friend encourages her to visit a psychologist and get treatment for her phobia. Anna wants to think about the suggestion.

PAC

Anna throws all her dog books in the trash. She bumps into Roman, who asks her if she now owns a dog. She tells him no and admits to her fear of dogs. Roman suggests she take part in anxiety-relieving confrontation therapy.

CPAC/Preparation

Anna books confrontation therapy. In the first therapy session, to ease Anna's fears, a muzzle encloses the jaws of a Dogo Argentino. The dog's name is *Butcher*.

CPAC

By the end of the first act, Anna has overcome her fear of dogs and takes the pit bull home with her from the shelter. She calls the dog *Destroy Them*, but all he wants to do all day is guard the sofa and sleep (*negative event* for Anna). What now? If you have drafted a sequence or act and have hit a wall and run out of ideas for scenes to push your story forward, use the story element system (SES) to sketch out the subsequent sequence or act — see chapter 2 for details.

3.3   As Good as it Gets

Using a short excerpt I call *Ride in a Garbage Chute* from the romcom *As Good as it Gets*, I will show how elements are used to give the excerpt structure.

00:29–01:53
NE: Simon Bishop's dog, Verdell, is running loose in the hallway. PAC (Melvin doesn't put his PAC into words): Melvin wants to get Verdell out of the hallway. CPAC: Melvin tries in vain to lure Verdell to the elevator. NE: Verdell pees in the hallway. ER: Melvin loses his cool. CPAC: Melvin throws Verdell in the garbage chute — *a character achieves his goal*. Five elements are used to tell this little story, which ends in a climax: Melvin dropping Verdell into the garbage chute. Resolution: Verdell is gone.

04:36–05:37
A character achieves his goal: Simon and Verdell are reunited. ER: Simon and Verdell are both ecstatic. NE: the janitor suggests that maybe some nice neighbor shoved Verdell down the garbage chute. PAC: Simon wants to talk to Melvin about the garbage chute incident (Simon doesn't put his PAC into words, but we can deduce it from the context in the scene).

05:37–08:30 (from Simon's point of view)
CPAC: Simon rings Melvin's doorbell and confronts him. NE for Simon: Melvin humiliates him. NE for Frank (Frank and Simon are very good friends): he hears and sees how Melvin verbally demeans Simon. PAC: Frank decides to give Melvin a piece of his mind and stop him from hurting Simon in the future. Frank doesn't voice his PAC.

05:37–08:30 (from Melvin's point of view)
NE: Simon interrupts Melvin while he's writing a novel. PAC: Melvin wants peace and quiet to work. CPAC: Melvin, humiliating Simon, makes it unequivocally clear that Simon is NOT to interrupt him while he's working.

08:30−09:48
CPAC: Frank berates Melvin, threatening him with physical violence. The *negative event* behind this CPAC takes place from 05:37 to 08:30: Frank hears and sees how Melvin demeans Simon. PAC: Frank wants to warn Melvin to never again treat Simon so disrespectfully. Frank doesn't voice his PAC.

Note
On page 102 (*Elements determine a character's personality*), I use *Ride in a Garbage Chute* to show how elements determine a character's personality.

3.4 Practice makes perfect

Separate the following story into its elements. The story is about two minutes long and consists of a single building block divided into four micros — see page 16—19 about micros. The overarching story in the building block: Pretty Janica is looking for her car key because she has to get to a crucial photo shoot.

Micro #1
Janica searches the house for her car key[1], but can't find it[2].

Micro #2
She complains[3] to her husband, Josip, because she thinks he has once again put the car key down somewhere it doesn't belong[4]. Janica is also furious[5] that Josip spends half the day playing *Assassin's Creed Odyssey* on the computer[6]. The breakdown of their marriage seems imminent[7].

Mikro #3

Then Janica hears the jingle of keys. She turns toward the source of the sound and sees an ugly pit bull terrier chewing on her car key. The dog, whose name is *Dog*, is Josip's best friend. Janica chases the dog through the house and retrieves her key.

Mikro #4

Janica hurries out to her Agent 47 Harbinger Mustang while Josip, who is carrying out the garbage, snaps at Janica, telling her that all she ever does is spread negative vibes. She pulls the car key out of her pants pocket and accidentally drops it down a storm drain. Josip laughs at his wife loud enough for the entire neighborhood to hear. Snarling "Mrzim te!" loudly, he slams the front door behind him and yells: "You can't drive anyway! And you can't cook, either! And you are ugly. And I love you . . . not." Janica kneels on the ground and reaches into the storm drain, but she can't reach the key. Clenching her teeth, she marches back to the house. Along the way, she angrily kicks a garden gnome. The gnome flies through the air and crashes onto the windscreen of a parked police car, in which officers Mateo and Matje are eating cevapcici. Startled, they throw their lunch in the air, spilling it all over themselves. Snorting furiously, the two officers climb out of their car and glare at Janica. Mateo produces a pair of handcuffs. Janica smiles in embarrassment and slips her wallet out of her jacket pocket.

Solution

1. CPAC; 2. NE; 3. ER; 4. NE; 5. ER; 6. NE; 7. PAC.

We can use the SES to analyze a story. When we divide a story into its elements, we learn something about its structure and how elements have been used, for example to generate suspense.

4

Some authors may have limited imagination but still want to write, for example, a thriller. They might then analyze the elements of existing thrillers to learn about the genre. However, it is crucial for writers to ask the right questions if they want their analyses to yield useful information.

ANALYSING STORIES

4.1 Using elements to analyze films

With the assistance of the story element system, I methodically work through a screenplay or film and analyze why it demonstrates either a flawed or outstanding structure:

1. Watch a bad film.
2. Analyze the reason for its failure: insufficiently developed characters; lack of suspense; lack of conflict; no questions and matching answers, etc.
3. Break the film down into its existing elements.
4. If you find that the film is flawed because of its existing elements, swap the elements that are not working for functioning ones you develop yourself specifically to improve the film. Then rewrite the original story until you've created a better version. For now, a synopsis is enough. Then post your version online, for example in a dedicated screenplay group on Facebook or Reddit, and ask for constructive feedback. This exercise sharpens your sense for the elements at work in your own screenplays.

Let's look at how we can utilize the story element system to analyze and revise a film, using *Wild Card* (2015) as an example. This represents only one way to analyze a film, of course.

Plot of Wild Card

Nick, a gambler and drinker, works as a bodyguard in Las Vegas. After his ex-girlfriend, hostess Holly, is assaulted by several men at the Golden Nugget Hotel, Holly asks Nick to track the men down. Nick, however, suspects that organized crime is behind Holly's assault, so he refuses to help her. When he then changes his mind and decides to help after all, his research quickly leads him to Danny, who assaulted Holly. Once Nick has overpowered Danny and his bodyguards, Nick and Holly take 50,000 dollars from Danny's apartment. Nick and Holly split the loot and Holly leaves the city. When Mafia boss and hotel owner "Baby" hears from Danny what happened, he brings Nick and Danny together and each tells his version of the story. When Danny tells his side, it becomes clear to Baby that Danny is lying, which is why Baby lets Nick go. But Danny can't let the matter rest, and with several of his men, he ambushes Nick. Nick, however, kills all of them. Let's take a look at the most important scenes (start of the movie until minute 33) from *Wild Card — Extended Cut*:

Wild Card (Extended Cut)

Start—14: we get to know Nick Wild, the main character. Nick harasses Doris in a bar. Osgood, Doris's boyfriend, enters the bar and the situation between the three escalates until Osgood berates Nick outside the bar and beats him up in front of Doris.

14—16: during the opening credits, someone dumps a severely injured Holly in front of a hospital. Holly is Nick's ex-girlfriend.

16—17: doctors at the hospital treat Holly and ask her who hurt her so badly.

17—23: Nick drives to Pinky's law office. Pinky shares the office with Nick, who works as a security consultant and bodyguard. Pinky reads out a couple of letters that have arrived for Nick (*). Cyrus Kinnick, a software millionaire, enters the office and wants to hire Nick to escort him through Las Vegas as a bodyguard (**). Through their conversation, we discover that Nick is trained in self-defense and is fluent in four languages. We also discover

that Nick is very good at lying, so we still don't know what's true
(*). Nick wants to meet with Cyrus Kinnick in the evening (**).

23—25: Osgood visits Nick and pays him for their staged encounter earlier at the bar — the two are friends. Osgood had
hired Nick to let Osgood beat him up because Osgood wanted
to play the brave guy in front of Doris (PAC). He recapitulates
to Nick how their little game came about, and reveals that he
achieved what he set out to achieve (*a character achieves his
goal*): that Doris wants to be with him. Start—14 thus plays
through Osgood's and Nick's CPAC; I won't pursue this any
further here because it plays no role in the rest of the film.

25—28: Nick visits his regular diner, where waitress Roxy serves
him coffee and juice (*). Nick tells Roxy that he needs five hundred thousand dollars for five free years (*). Roxy tells Nick that
Holly called for him and wants to see him (**).

28—33: Nick visits Holly, who tells him that some men assaulted
her, which we see in short flashbacks (*). Nick wants to go after
the men (**).

Break the individual scenes down into elements

To make sure things don't get too complicated, we subdivide
start—33 only into the most important elements. By breaking the
story into categories, we obtain an overview at a glance — this
approach simplifies thinking about the elements:

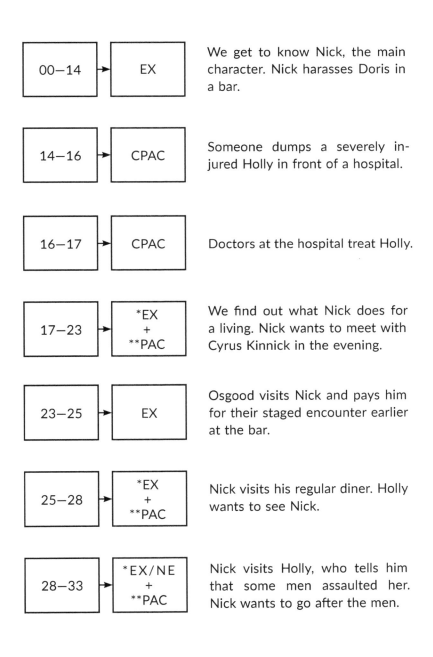

00—14	→	EX	We get to know Nick, the main character. Nick harasses Doris in a bar.
14—16	→	CPAC	Someone dumps a severely injured Holly in front of a hospital.
16—17	→	CPAC	Doctors at the hospital treat Holly.
17—23	→	*EX + **PAC	We find out what Nick does for a living. Nick wants to meet with Cyrus Kinnick in the evening.
23—25	→	EX	Osgood visits Nick and pays him for their staged encounter earlier at the bar.
25—28	→	*EX + **PAC	Nick visits his regular diner. Holly wants to see Nick.
28—33	→	*EX/NE + **PAC	Nick visits Holly, who tells him that some men assaulted her. Nick wants to go after the men.

Below is a modified version of the period covered in start—33. I've changed the arrangement (structure) of the various scenes because their present structure creates very little suspense. Also, the dialogues contain too much exposition.

Modified version
Start—3: Two cops question Nick, who tells them that it's his job as a bodyguard to protect his clients from drunken idiots. In the background, firefighters are cutting three of these idiots free, they are taped to a lamppost with duct tape. A fourth idiot is stuck to the lamppost four meters above the ground. The tape tears and the poor guy lands on the police car like a wet sack, crying for his mother.

3—6: While Nick drives home in his 67 Mustang, he calls his regular diner and asks Roxy to give his breakfast to Horst, a homeless guy — the altercation earlier has spoiled Nick's appetite. Roxy takes Nick's breakfast across to Horst, who is begging for money from passersby on the other side of the street. Nick arrives home, lies down, and goes to sleep, but his neighbors Susan and Jim soon wake him up with a furious argument because there's no milk in the fridge while the radio plays *Into the Groove* from Madonna. Nick is unable to calm his neighbors down, so he elects to sleep in his car instead.

6—9: Nick picks Cyrus Kinnick up from his hotel and escorts him through a night in Las Vegas. Cyrus gambles in a casino.

9—11: When Nick goes to a bar with Cyrus, they run into Holly, who is on her way to a party with girlfriends. Nick implores Holly to look after herself.

11–13: By early the next morning, Cyrus is drunk and Nick takes him back to his hotel before going to the diner for breakfast. Nick tells Roxy that he needs five hundred thousand dollars for five free years.

13–16: Holly leaves the party but is waylaid at the hotel elevator by gangster Danny, assaulted and dumped seriously injured in front of the hospital.

16–17: Doctors treat Holly at the hospital.

17–19: Nick pays Roxy for breakfast and leaves the diner, switching off his mobile phone because he wants some peace and quiet. After he's left, Holly calls Roxy and tells her that Nick has to go by her apartment. Roxy hurries out of the diner after Nick, but he is nowhere to be seen. He is talking with Horst, who is counting his change in a side street. As Nick is handing him twenty dollars, Roxy finds him and passes on the message that Holly urgently wants to see him.

19–21: Nick visits Holly, who tells him about the abuse she has suffered – without flashbacks. Nick wants to make the men who hurt Holly pay for it.

Compare the two versions

To be better able to compare the two versions, we put them side by side in a graphic. For the modified version of the story, I'm using only the most important elements; nevertheless, building block 17–19, for example, contains multiple elements:

Original version:

Note: I delete the exposition (EX) in start—14 and 23—25, because they add nothing of importance to the story.

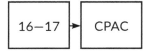

Someone dumps a severely injured Holly in front of a hospital.

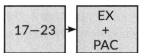

Doctors at the hospital treat Holly.

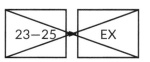

chapter
04

We find out what Nick does for a living. Nick wants to meet with Cyrus Kinnick in the evening.

Nick visits his regular diner. Holly wants to see Nick.

Nick visits Holly, who tells him that some men assaulted her. Nick wants to go after the men.

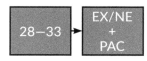

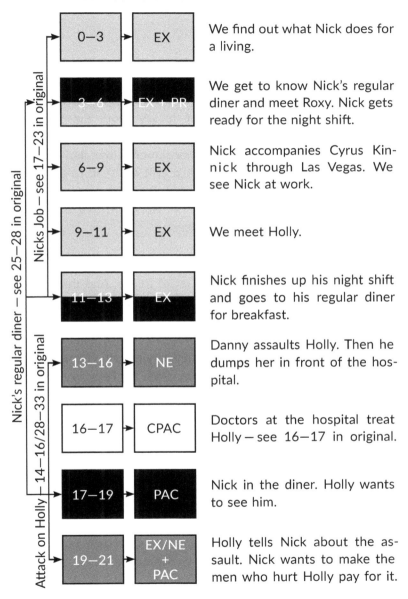

Modified version:

0–3	EX	We find out what Nick does for a living.
3–6	EX + PR	We get to know Nick's regular diner and meet Roxy. Nick gets ready for the night shift.
6–9	EX	Nick accompanies Cyrus Kinnick through Las Vegas. We see Nick at work.
9–11	EX	We meet Holly.
11–13	EX	Nick finishes up his night shift and goes to his regular diner for breakfast.
13–16	NE	Danny assaults Holly. Then he dumps her in front of the hospital.
16–17	CPAC	Doctors at the hospital treat Holly – see 16–17 in original.
17–19	PAC	Nick in the diner. Holly wants to see him.
19–21	EX/NE + PAC	Holly tells Nick about the assault. Nick wants to make the men who hurt Holly pay for it.

Nicks Job – see 17–23 in original

Nick's regular diner – see 25–28 in original

Attack on Holly – 14–16/28–33 in original

4.2   The value of film analysis

An effective method of learning about writing screenplays is to analyze films. Analyze the genre in which you want to write your story. Watch, for example, several different thrillers. Compare them. Read what film critics have to say about these thrillers. Read one-star reviews on IMDb, Amazon or Rotten Tomatoes and learn from the mistakes of other screenwriters and directors. Listen to what Jean-Michel Basquiat († 1988) had to say about analyzing art. Works by Jean-Michel Basquiat are among the most expensive by any US artist. His work *Untitled* from 1982 sold in 2017 for 110.5 million dollars.

"I never went to an art school. I failed the art courses that I did take in school. I just looked at a lot of things. And that's how I learnt about art, by looking at it." *Jean-Michel Basquiat*

We will analyze several scenes from *Jaws* (thriller) and *Enemy of the State* (thriller) to find out about why certain elements were used to tell the story in each film. Both thrillers are perfectly structured and suspenseful.

4.3   Jaws — Act 1 (start—21)

BB 01:11—02:22 (ER + PAC)
ER: Chrissie and other students are having fun at a beach party. PAC: Chrissie wants to go for a swim, which we only hear from her in the following BB. Note: NE: maybe Chrissie is bored. PAC: that's probably why she wants to go swimming.

BB 02:22−03:27 (PR + CPAC)
PR: Chrissie runs down to the water and strips off her clothes.
CPAC: Chrissie swims in the sea.

BB 03:27−04:55 (NE)
A great white shark attacks and kills Chrissie.

BB 04:55−06:49 (PAC)
Brody wants to check the remains discovered on the beach.

BB 06:49−08:33 (CPAC)
Brody drives to the beach and checks the remains.

BB 08:33−09:14 (NE + PAC)
NE: on the phone, Brody learns that a shark killed Chrissie. PAC:
Brody wants to close the beach.

BB 09:14−11:05 (PR)
Brody buys what he needs to close the beach.

BB 11:05−13:03 (A character does not achieve his goal)
Brody doesn't achieve his goal of closing the beach.

BB 13:03−15:55 (EX)
People on the beach. We meet the Kintner family.

BB 15:55−17:28 (NE)
The shark kills Alex Kintner.

The building block 17:28–19:45 consists of four micros:

Micro 17:28–17:59 (PAC)
Mrs. Kintner wants someone to kill the shark.

Micro 17:59–18:31
See *Practice makes perfect* on page 18.

Micro 18:31–18:57
See *Practice makes perfect* on page 19.

Micro 18:57–19:45 (PAC)
Brody talks to the citizens and wants to take action, including closing the beach.

BB 19:45–21:39 (EX + CPAC)
EX: we get to know Quint. CPAC: citizens close the beach.

A short analysis

Before the shark attack on Chrissie, a beach party is taking place. To elicit an emotional reaction from viewers with BB 15–17, I swap the beach party for the *Delicious Dinner* scene I've developed. Delicious Dinner scene: Chrissie takes her dog, Delicious Dinner, for a walk along the beach. Delicious Dinner jumps into the water and does not reappear, which causes to Chrissie to venture into the water to look for the little mutt. Because a small dog isn't enough to satisfy a shark, the shark eats Chrissie, too. But what purpose does the Delicious Dinner scene serve? It gives more suspense to the *Pipit* scene in BB 15–17. Pipit is a dog that disappears in the sea (he also serves as an appetizer for the shark) and whose owner look for him before the shark kills Alex. If viewers are confronted with Pipit's disappearance, they will be reminded of Delicious Dinner, who also disappeared in the sea, just before the shark killed Chrissie. Which emotional reaction does the combination of the Delicious Dinner and Pipit scenes elicit in the viewer? The Pipit scene creates extreme suspense in a viewer before the attack on Alex because people are in the water in BB 15–17 and the viewer, because of Pipit's disappearance, suspects that the shark is close by. But then why was a party set up to start the film? For one thing, it establishes a sharp contrast with the shark attack on Chrissie. The film also relies on a shock-and-surprise moment in BB 15–17.

An observation to BB 13:03–15:55

Which element of a building block is the main element? In BB 13–15, the most important element for the ongoing development of the story is that we get to know Mrs. Kintner and her son Alex, who will be killed by the shark in the following building block. Practice makes perfect: Analyze movies and ask yourself how you can rewrite irrelevant elements into elements useful to the story.

4.4   Enemy of the State – Act 1 (start–21)

BB 00–03 (CPAC + NE)
CPAC: Thomas Reynolds attempts to persuade Phil Hammersley about a piece of legislation that Hammersley doesn't want to support (NE for Reynolds).

BB 03–04 (CPAC)
Reynolds's people kill Hammersley at the lake.

04—06
Opening credits.

BB 06—07 (NE + PAC)
NE: the Mafia is causing problems. PAC: Dean therefore wants to sit down and talk with the Mafia.

BB 07—09 (EX)
We meet Rachel and Brill and learn about Brill's working relationship with Dean and Rachel.

BB 09—11 (CPAC + NE)
CPAC: Dean talks with the Mafia. NE: Pintero finds out that someone has secretly made a video of him.

chapter
04

BB 11—13 (PAC/NE)
Pintero wants to know who made the video of him or he'll kill Dean. Pintero's PAC is a *negative event* for Dean.

BB 13—15 (NE)
Bingham discovers that Zavitz videoed Hammersley's murder.

The building block 15:20—17:27 consists of four micros:

> Micro 15:20—15:42 (PAC)
> Hicks goes to Thomas Reynolds because he wants to inform him about the murder video.

> Micro 15:42—16:18 (CPAC; NE)
> Hicks tells Reynolds about the murder video — a *negative event + exposition* for Reynolds.

Micro 16:18–16:58 (PAC)
Reynolds wants the video.

Micro 16:58–17:27 (PR)
Hicks orders a wiretap on Zavitz. Reynolds's men recruit ex-Marines.

BB 17–19 (NE + PAC)
EX for Zavitz/NE for Reynolds: Zavitz sees the murder on the video and informs Bloom. PAC: Reynolds wants Zavitz watched.

BB 19–21 (PR)
Preparations for Christmas: Dean buys Christmas presents.

A short analysis
Enemy of the State wastes no time, introducing us to the characters in scenes that are important for the development of the story. Let's ask a question about Hammersley: why is there no emotional reaction to Hammersley's death? Because we don't meet anyone from his family or circle of friends who could grieve his death — Hammersley is just an accessory to push the story along. Also, no scene in which a character mourns the death of another would fit in this thriller. Such a mourning scene would destroy the mood and take the pace out of the story.

Screenwriters can doubtless show family members grieving for a dead character, even if we only meet the family after the character's death. But if scriptwriters want to entertain the audience with an ER, they logically additionally add a scene that shows the deceased with members of his family or with friends before his death, as in the scene in *Jaws* where Mrs. Kintner talks to her son Alex (BB 13—15) — without this scene, Mrs. Kintner's grief in BB 34—36 carries little emotional entertainment value for the viewer. For every element employed, writers ask themselves: what purpose does this element serve in my story?

Let's study the elements used to structure the micro 15:42—16:18 (Reynolds finds out about the murder video). For Hicks, this micro is a CPAC, but for Reynolds it's a *negative event + exposition*. Micros are explained on page 16 below.

Micro 15:42—16:18

CPAC
Hicks enters Reynolds's office because Hicks wants (PAC) to inform Reynolds about the murder video.

Exposition
We get to know Reynolds's office. Reynolds makes a telephone call (story filler [SF]), from which we learn that he hates optimism (EX). Then he hangs up.

Exposition
Hicks takes a remote control and switches on a monitor. On the monitor, we see information about Zavitz, a nature photographer. Hicks tells Reynolds that there is a problem at the lake where the murder took place. He takes a seat in front of Reynolds's desk and explains who Zavitz is, what he does for a living, and that he . . .

Negative event + exposition for Reynolds
. . . filmed the murder at the lake.

The End of Chapter Four

With the aid of several examples, I will show how writers can make their work easier by using the SES.

5

The more intensively writers engage with the story element system, the more ideas they develop about how to use the SES as a creativity technique in order to make their work easier.

TIPS & TRICKS

5.1   Developing elements from newspaper reports

A fictional newspaper article: because of a broken cellphone, a father kills his son and goes into hiding. The police launch a manhunt. Police helicopters fly over the site. Officers with trained dogs search the adjoining forest. We break this report down into its elements: NE: the father kills his son. PAC: the father wants to go into hiding. CPAC: he hides in the woods. This CPAC is an NE for the police, who develop a PAC of their own in response to this negative catastrophe: they decide to hunt the father down. CPAC: the police launch their manhunt. Looking back at the broken cellphone, we develop the story that precedes it. We also divide this into its elements: NE: the son destroys his gambling-addicted father's smartphone, at the same time destroying his game scores, which were saved on the phone. ER: the father loses his cool and zaps his son with a Taser. But his son has a pacemaker implanted in his chest. NE: the son dies of a heart attack. For the son, destroying the phone is a CPAC in response to the NE of his father ruining the family financially with his gambling addiction.

chapter
05

5.2   Using plausible elements

What does a plausible action look like? A plausible action is one that anyone would think of. Little creativity is required for this. With the following technique, writers should not use the first action/element that comes to mind. If writers find no ideas to push their story forward, they break their existing actions down into elements and look for new elements that follow plausibly. Fictional example: Kacper and his butler Wojciech get into a shootout with the Mafia. NE: a bullet hits Kacper. Plausible element to follow this NE? An ER: Kacper and Wojciech are worried about Kacper's injury. A PAC follows: Wojciech wants to get Kacper to a hospital. How can we aggravate their situation? With an NE: Kacper and Wojciech are in the middle of nowhere and there isn't a hospital anywhere nearby. A plausible element to follow this NE? A PAC: emergency operation in the middle of nowhere. CPAC: performing the emergency operation. NE: Kacper dies on the operating table. A plausible element in response to Kacper's death? ER: Wojciech's grief at Kacper's death + Kacper's funeral + Wojciech's fury at the murder. After this, we might use a PAC: Wojciech wants revenge. CPAC? The CPAC depends on the character's personality. A courageous character might get his hands on a gun and ambush Kacper's killers. A more anxious character might go to the police or hire hit woman Adelajda. What plausible element would follow if Wojciech hires Adelajda? CPAC: Adelajda tries to carry out her contract. NE for Adelajda: her target captures her, and she throws Wojciech under the bus.

5.3   Detecting development faults

To detect faults in story development, writers reduce their story to the elements that drive it forward. But how do we know if and how a story is continuing to develop? What markers are there? In BB 36—37 in *Jaws*, Martin Brody is depressed because he feels responsible for the death of Alex Kintner. This ER certainly adds something to the story, but it does not drive it forward like the NE in BB 39—41: Hooper informs Brody that the killer shark is still alive. Brody and Hooper react to this *negative event* with a PAC: they want to cut open the tiger shark. CPAC:

Hooper cuts open the tiger shark. NE, PAC and CPAC drive the story forward — it continues to develop.

5.4   Using elements to stretch a story

Elements are excellent for the much-maligned technique of story-stretching. Each of the elements can be used as story-stretcher (story filler [SF]). But take care: excessive use of this technique should be avoided. An example: Klara wants to buy teabags in the supermarket (PAC). We stretch the scene with the *preparation* element: Klara combs her hair and sprays a little Poison eau de toilette on her neck. She slips on her shoes — Gucci — then changes to a pair of Louis Vuitton. Klara cuts short a call from her mother, who, to improve her German skills, wants to grouch to Klara in German about a cigar-smoking neighbor. Stretching the screenplay in this way gives the future film director an extra fifty seconds of material to work with. This preparation scene does not put viewers off — the story-stretching remains unnoticed, because everyone knows what it's like to get ready to leave the house, even if they're wearing sneakers and not Louis Vuitton. Practice makes perfect: find a story-stretcher that reveals something about the personality of a character. Klara's ultra-obsession with beauty might indicate that she ignores her emotional needs.

Find the mistake
NE: the shark kills Chrissie.
NE: they discover Chrissie's remains.
PAC: Brody wants to check the remains discovered on the beach.
CPAC: Brody checks the remains.

ER: Brody eats a burger with the works to help him process the terrible images in his head.
ER: Brody talks about his misery with a friend.
NE: on the phone, Brody learns that a shark killed Chrissie.
ER: Mrs. Brody screams at Martin because he missed lunch.
The *burger, friend, marital issues* scenes slow down the story. Again, excessive use of story-stretching is to be avoided. The genre of your story will help when deciding when to use which elements to tell (or stretch) the story.

5.5 Devising entertaining elements for a climax

In *Jaws*, BB 21—23 doesn't contain any kind of *negative event* or any other element that both *drives the story forward* and also *entertains* the viewer. What did the screenwriters add to improve this building block? A climax: Afraid that the shark could attack his son's boat any second, Brody snaps at Michael to get out of the boat immediately. Mrs. Brody, who is more relaxed about the matter, reassures her husband. However, she knows nothing about how capable of attacking small boats a shark is. Climax: leafing through a book about sharks, she sees a picture of a shark attacking a small boat (the viewer also sees this photo for the first time), she suddenly loses her cool and screams at Michael to get out of the boat. The point of this scene is to make the audience worry. Mrs. Brody's *emotional reaction* forms one part of the tension in this scene, while the shark photo (and Michael in the boat) forms the other.

BB 23—26: in the evening, wanting to lure the shark, Denherder and Charlie take their boat to a jetty. Charlie threads a chunk of meat onto a hook attached to a chain and wraps the chain around one of the jetty's pylons. Then he tosses the baited hook into the water and waits on the jetty with Denherder, who is whistling a tune. The shark takes the bait and pulls the chain so hard that part of the wooden jetty collapses. Charlie falls into the water, landing on the section of the broken jetty that the shark is dragging out to sea. Charlie is swimming back to the destroyed jetty when the broken section turns back and follows Charlie — now the shark is hunting him. Charlie reaches the broken jetty and tries to climb up, but keeps slipping back into the water . . . while the shark is getting closer and closer. This well-structured building block plays with viewers' expectations and delivers considerable suspense with its climax. The climax brings together two CPACs: the shark goes after Charlie. Charlie tries to escape.

BB 6–8 in *Blood Diamond*: RUF prisoners search for diamonds in a diamond mine. Climax: a prisoner finds a diamond (*positive event*/positive catastrophe) and hides it in his mouth (CPAC), but is spotted by Captain Poison (NE for the prisoner), who demands the diamond back. The prisoner hands the diamond to Poison, who then shoots him dead. This climax does not push the story forward — the climax serves to entertain (shock) viewers and to show that, for Captain Poison, a human life means nothing.

BB 8–11 ends with Archer *achieving his goal*: he exchanges Coetzee's weapons for diamonds. In what way does achieving this goal drive the story forward? Because Archer wants to take the diamonds he's obtained to Coetzee (PAC), which is why he's marching toward the border in BB 11–13 (CPAC). Achieving his goal (a simple exchange of goods) at the end of BB 8–11

contains no great entertainment value for the viewer. The entertainment for the viewers happens at the start of the building
block: Archer is dropped off by airplane and gets into a conflict
with Captain Rambo. Rambo stops Archer from going any farther
(CPAC for Rambo, NE for Archer).

BB 11–13: Archer sews Coetzee's diamonds beneath the skin of
several goats (PR) and smuggles them across the border (CPAC).
Climax: soldiers stop Archer at the border (NE for Archer), examine the goats (CPAC), and find the diamonds (NE for Archer, *goal
achieved* for the soldiers). Resolution: the soldiers arrest Archer.
The climax and resolution both drive the story forward, as well
as fulfilling the task of entertaining the audience.

5.6   Using elements to title a scene

We divide a film into acts, acts into sequences, sequences
into units, units into building blocks, and building blocks into
micros – see pages 16–19. A building block, as a rule, consists
of four micros. A micro comprises several elements that tell the
story in the micro. One of these micros contains the most important element of the building block, and we use this element
as the building block title. BB 29–31 in *Jaws* consists of four
micros: 29:46–30:09–30:40–31:12–31:27. The final micro
contains the most important of the building block's element, and
we take this as the **title** of the building block: **NE**: Hooper announces that it was a shark that killed Chrissie. When we break
down segments such as acts, sequences, units, etc. into elements, we can see whether we have used a balance of elements
to create variety in the story. In the following example – about

a fictional musical duo who, by the end of the example, each goes his own way — I demonstrate how you can use an element to title a micro or building block.

1 Micro   PAC
Emma, Jonas's girlfriend, wants Jonas to wear a base-ball cap with *Emma* printed on it for an upcoming music video. This PAC, however, is a *negative event* for Karl, the other half of the duo.

2 Micro   A character does not achieve his goal
Emma and Karl get into a discussion because crazy Emma is interfering with the duo's business and insists on the baseball cap.

3 Micro   PAC
ER: Karl breaks down in tears in front of the music video director and drinks a glass of warm milk with honey. PAC: the director recommends that Karl disband the duo.

4 Micro   negative event ——————— BB-title ——————
                   Karl disbands the duo.

building block 15–17

N
E

Emma's insistence on seeing the baseball cap in the video repre-sents a *negative event* for Karl, and he reacts to this with a PAC: he wants to talk Emma out of the idea. But in the subsequent CPAC, *Karl does not achieve his goal* — a negative catastrophe for him. You can determine which element you choose for the title of a micro based on which element drives the story for-ward — a micro usually consists of several.

In Micro 1, the focus is on what Emma wants. For this micro, I choose the element PAC as my title, although Emma's will signifies a serious *negative event* for Karl and is the reason Karl wants to discuss the baseball cap with Emma (PAC).

Micro 2 contains two elements. CPAC: Karl tries to convince Emma that the baseball cap doesn't belong in the video. *A character does not achieve his goal*: for Emma, it's non-negotiable. She wants to see a baseball cap with her name on it in the video or the shoot is over. Because Karl's negative catastrophe of *not achieving his goal* carries more weight than the discussion between him and Emma (CPAC), I call this micro *a character does not achieve his goal*.

The third micro contains an ER (Karl breaks down in tears and drinks warm milk with a lot of honey) and a PAC (Karl wants to dissolve the duo with Jonas). Karl's PAC is the most important element in micro 3, because it is Karl's will here that pushes the story onward.

The fourth micro contains the CPAC. At the same time, this CPAC represents a *negative event* (a single action can consist of several elements): Karl disbands the duo. This *negative event* is the most important and consequential element in the building block and is therefore used as the building block title.

Note
The form of a CPAC or any other element plays a fundamental role in entertaining viewers, and also determines the genre. As entertainment, throwing a cream pie into a politician's face is different from throwing the politician off the 17th floor of a

high-rise building. In the right circumstances, however, viewers could find the high-rise politician toss liberating or even funny — it all depends on the context.

5.7 Elements determine a character's personality

Elements structure not only stories, but also reveal something about a character. Let's take a look at the characters in *As Good as it Gets*. But before continuing, take another look at *Ride in a Garbage Chute* on page 70.

Simon

What does Simon's PAC (he wants to confront Melvin for throwing Verdell down the garbage chute) tell us about him? Why does he chose this PAC? His PAC gives us the impression that Simon is the type of person who defends his honor. What does Simon's CPAC reveal about his character? Simon is not able to assert himself.

Melvin

What does Melvin's PAC (he wants his peace and quiet so he can work [he's trying to write his next novel] — a common PAC) and his CPAC tell us about him? Melvin rebukes Simon in the most obnoxious terms and makes it crystal clear to him that he is not to disturb his work under any circumstances. Melvin's CPAC reveals to us that he's a blunt, hateful human being who doesn't care at all about other people's feelings.

Frank

What does Frank's PAC tell us about Frank? That he looks after his friends. He wants to warn Melvin to never treat Simon badly again. What does Frank's CPAC reveal about his character? He is assertive, he is able to intimidate people, and he leans toward physical violence.

Causes of a character's behavior

Often, we find the root of a particular PAC/CPAC in a character's past. Why can't Simon assert himself? What has he experienced in the past? What role does his upbringing play in his lack of assertiveness? Why is Melvin so hateful and so insensitive to other people's feelings? What past did Melvin suffer through to make him behave so horribly toward other people (whether consciously or unconsciously), just to keep them at a distance? His behavior demonstrates that he wants nothing to do with other people. But why? Why does Frank look after his friends? And why is he inclined toward physical violence? What events in his past have shaped his present-day behavior?

Attitude

PAC and CPAC also reveal something about a character's attitude and how they feel about a particular matter. If a character uses e.g. violence (a method) to achieve a goal (e.g. intimidating migrants), what does this method reveal about the character? That he or she is crude and primitive — see *American History X*.

5.8   Creating a how-can-I-use-elements list

— Combine elements: Hans yells (ER) philosophically (PH) at his employees.
— Change the setting: the scene takes place not in an auto

repair shop, but at the zoo.

— Replace suitable elements for "unsuitable ones".
— Exaggerate elements: in his anger, Hans gets in a car and runs over his employee.
— Replace elements with others: we change the CPAC element (Máté buys bread rolls) into the element *a character achieves her goal*. Before that, Máté and Nóra discuss who should buy the rolls. The discussion is Nóra's CPAC to follow the PAC that Nóra doesn't want to go out for rolls. She's expecting Péter to call on their landline — he wants to talk with Máté (NE #1) because he beat Nóra the previous day (NE #2). This NE #1 for Nóra is a PAC for Péter in response to NE #2.
— You can extend the list as far as you want to.

5.9   Arranging elements in a category system

We take all of the PACs that trigger a subsequent act and put them in the category of act-triggering PACs. Let's look at the act-triggering PACs from *Jaws*: 17: Mrs. Kintner wants someone to kill the shark — this PAC (+ shark kills Alex) triggers the second act. 63: Brody wants to kill the shark in open waters — this PAC (+ shark kills man) triggers the third act. 106: Hooper wants to poison the shark — this PAC (+ boat's motor explodes) triggers the fourth act. Now we analyze these PACs: do they increase in intensity? Are they too similar to each other? Does the risk to the characters grow with each PAC? Do the PACs being used increase the suspense? We do this analysis for each element and create a category system in which we organize each of the elements we've utilized: we arrange ER scenes into the ER category, all of the *exposition* into the EXPOSITION category, all *negative events* into the NEGATIVE EVENTS category, etc. Then we ask questions to find out how we can improve the elements we have used to tell the story.

5.10   Developing a screenplay at a glance

For this, we need a large monitor. We create four sections consisting of four graphics. Each section represents one act. Then we divide each act into building blocks. Each BB occupies a writable column beneath the act: start—3—5—7—9—11 etc. We then write the scenes we've developed into the building-block columns, which we can shorten or lengthen as required. If we think of a scene for the fourth act, we enter this into the building-block column for that act. In this way, the acts fill with scenes. If we zoom out from the overall graphic occasionally, we can see all of the scenes at once and consider the story as a whole. Seeing all of a story's scenes at a glance allows us to compare scenes with other scenes more efficiently, for example to assess whether a particular scene is too weak or too strong at a certain point, or perhaps needs to be altered because we just changed a scene in act 4. When you look at your graphic, you can ask yourself certain questions, such as does the story intensify, do the actions get more exciting, do the catastrophes get worse for the characters, etc. Take a look at the graphic on the next page, where I give an example.

Logline
Four homeless people live on the streets of Los Angeles and believe they live in hell until they meet a super-rich sociopath and his barbaric friends, people even Alex DeLarge would fear.

Writable columns based on building blocks. These can be shortened or lengthened as desired and combined to form units or sequences.

ACT 1

Unit 00—04:

11:23 pm: Alexander is enjoying a party with friends in his mansion. We learn about Alexander's sadistic character. Fabian and Carlos are Alexander's best friends. Brigitte is Alexander's girlfriend. They want to go downtown to relax from the party.

BB 04—07:

Oliver, Bastian, Chris and Max are homeless and live under a bridge. Some drunk guys attack them, just for fun. Oliver and his friends have no fighting skills and get their butts kicked.

BB 07—09:

Oliver and his friends go to the police, but the cops don't want to help them. Oliver is depressed because life always seems to be screwing them over. Oliver goes downtown alone.

BB 09—11:

Oliver begs for money downtown. Most of the people don't give a damn about him. A dog pees on him. The dog's owner laughs his head off.

ACT 3

ACT 4

ACT 1 . . .

BB 11–13:

Oliver looks through the window of the exclusive Ketsueki bistro and observes Alexander, Brigitte, Fabian and Carlos having a good time. The door-man argues with Oliver and sends him away. As he leaves, Alexander goes to his black Mercedes.

BB 13–15:

Oliver is sitting on a bench and observes Alexander and his friends walking down the street. When Oliver steals Brigitte's handbag, she falls and breaks her arm. Oliver flees. Alexander and his friends chase Oliver, who escapes. He searches the handbag and finds Brigitte's ID and a membership card from the Evil Clown Club. The ID says that Brigitte lives in Beverly Hills. He puts the ID and member-ship card back into the handbag. A homeless woman observes how Oliver takes the money out of Brigitte's wallet. He throws the bag away. The woman takes the handbag.

BB 15–17:

Alexander, Fabian and Carlos are in hospital. A doctor takes care of Brigitte's arm. Alexander and his friends decide to find Oliver and take revenge. They don't want to go to the police.

The End of Chapter Five

List of films analyzed

"I never went to an art school. I failed the art courses that I did take in school. I just looked at a lot of things. And that's how I learnt about art, by looking at it." *Jean-Michel Basquiat*

Analyze the genre in which you want to write your story. If you want to write a comedy, analyze comedies that are similar to yours. One goal of your analysis could be, for example, to find out more about the style of humor used in the comedy. Note: if you write a comedy always remember to write it in such a way that the audience laughs their heads off. If you want to create a memorable villain, focus your film analysis on villains. The following is a listing of the films I have analyzed to develop the story element system and write this book:

American History X. Directed by Tony Kaye. Written by David McKenna. Release date 1998 USA.

A Prayer for the Dying. Directed by Mike Hodges. Written by Jack Higgins, Edmund Ward, Martin Lynch. Release date 1987 USA.

As Good as It Gets. Directed by James L. Brooks. Screenplay by Mark Andrus, James L. Brooks. Release date 1997 USA.

Blood Diamond. Directed by Edward Zwick. Written by Charles Leavitt. Release date 2006 USA.

Casablanca. Directed by M. Curtiz. Screenplay by Julius Epstein, Philip Epstein, Howard Koch. Release date 1942 USA.

Kick-Ass. Directed by Matthew Vaughn. Screenplay by Jane Goldman, Matthew Vaughn. Release date 2010 GB, USA.

The Matrix. Directed by The Wachowski Sisters. Written by The Wachowski Sisters. Release date 1999 USA, AUS.

Midnight Run. Directed by Martin Brest. Written by George Gallo. Release date 1988 USA.

Pulp Fiction. Directed by Quentin Tarantino. Written by Quentin Tarantino. Release date 1994 USA.

Enemy of the State. Directed by Tony Scott. Written by David Marconi. Release date 1998 USA.

Jaws. Directed by Steven Spielberg. Screenplay by Peter Benchley, Carl Gottlieb. Release date 1975 USA.

The Rundown. Directed by Peter Berg. Screenplay by R. J. Steward, James Vanderbilt. Release date 2003 USA.

Wild Card. Directed by Simon West. Screenplay by William Goldman. Release date 2015 France, USA.

Back to the Future. Directed by Robert Zemeckis. Written by Robert Zemeckis, Bob Gale. Release date 1985 USA.

Hasta la vista, baby!

Milton Keynes UK
Ingram Content Group UK Ltd.
UKHW020802080823
426520UK00015B/612